EDITED BY LISA LOWRIE

First published in Great Britain in 2017 by:

Forward Poetry

Remus House
Coltsfoot Drive
Peterborough
PE2 9BF
Telephone: 01733 890099
Website: www.forwardpoetry.co.uk

FOREWORD

At Forward Poetry our aim is to encourage and challenge poetic minds and provide them with a bridge to publication and a wider audience to appreciate their work. As such we regularly supply inspiring themes that are open to interpretation in order to spark the creative process and get writers to put pen to paper.

Our latest theme was eternal love, a topic that poets have wrestled with for generations. The result is a varied and heartfelt anthology of verse that encapsulates the love we have for our partners, parents, children and friends. There are joyous celebrations of those that enrich our lives and poignant odes to those sadly no longer with us.

This collection is full of emotion and touching personal experiences and is sure to provide inspiration for readers for years to come.

CONTENTS

Stuart Wells	115	Nina Thilo	161
Simon Warren	116	K Mork	162
Alison M Bass-Hunt	118	Sam Grant	163
Jade Kelly	120	Sian Cheung	164
Anthony Robert Aked	121	Sonakshi Mittal	165
Robert Barker	122	Christine Carol Burrows	166
Frank Flower	123	Brenda Maple	167
David Eager	124	Matt Humphries	168
Simon Maddrell	125	Kerry Summers	169
Carolie Cole Pemberton	126	Mutley	170
Lucie Prosser	127	Sue Gerrard	171
Priya Yoganathan	128	Robert Stevens	172
Sue Mullinger	129	Gareth Greer	173
Hilary Ankers	130	Shirley Walsh	174
Anita Wakeham	131	Terri-Ann Hammond	175
Susan Olivia Leyton Underhill	132	Joanna Murdoch	176
Adrian Bullard	133	Edna Sparkes	177
Leanne Drain	134	Roya Alsopp	178
Nina Graham	135	Martin F Holmes	179
Lorraine DeSousa	136	Jessica Stephanie Powell	180
Jonathan Lais	137	Muhammad Khurram Salim	181
Caitlin Coulson	138	Sara Nadeen Ashbourne	182
Samantha Shelford	139	Stella M Thompson	183
Christopher Sleeman	140	Kunjan Thankey	184
Yasemin Balandi	141	Trudie Sullivan	185
Edward Lyon	142	André Straker-Brown	186
PoGem	143	Mark Shaw	187
Jonathan Bryant	144	Liba Ravindran	188
Jean Cable	145	Gary Smith	189
Sammi	146	Paul Billett	190
Daniel Link	147	Ben Connor	191
Don Woods	148	Stella M Thompson	192
Imogen Swash	149	Jean Aked	193
Rebekah Hoare-Bond	150	Carla Dible	194
Tracy Davidson	151	Erica Kirk	195
Susan Kaye	152		
Mary Anne Moore	153		
Mustafa Al-Maree	154		
Katharine Goda	155		
Paula Holdstock	156		
Kierran Garner	157		
Denis Bruce	158		
David Babatunde Wilson	159		
Philippa Elmhirst	160		

THE POEMS

A LOVE IS LIKE NO OTHER

A love is like no other when you cannot let it go,
When the strings attached become detached but still it takes the blow.
When the link into the realms of palms becomes a distant wing,
But the memory can hit you with the deepest strongest sting.

A love is like no other when the death becomes your life,
When the overwhelming fear seems to strangle you at night,
But the love is tinged with crispy cream and scattered orange dust,
And the particles they spread on you like floating glitter bugs.

A love is like no other when the world has washed its hands,
When it's crushed you into pieces as they swell inside your glands,
Yet carefully you're sculpted from this impossible druggy mess,
Into a masterpiece by the one who never left.

A love is like no other when the depth becomes your soul,
When the peace resounds in all compounds and doesn't take control,
When contentment fills the parts of you and makes you feel restored,
Yet you feel like there is so much left to further be explored.

A love is like no other when the kidney becomes your own,
When the sacrifice becomes a want and not a need alone.
When the life support is holding the crutches to your yearn,
And you spend the days compiling how to take the sudden burn.

A love is like no other when you learn to say goodbye,
Because you know that they will sleep without that painful cry,
And even though your heart it weeps a piece of you will be,
Always scattered with the one who loved you indefinitely.

Jennifer Carrie Day

LOVE

I never knew what I was getting into when we met for the first time,
Never planned on romance, nothing further from my mind.
Unsure of where I stood in the relationship at hand,
Searching for myself amongst people who just didn't understand.
I never needed complications; I never asked for help, it's true.
I never looked for love that day, In fact I only looked at you.
Nothing was said, no words were uttered, we had a laugh and we had fun,
I never planned for love, I was already with someone.
That week flew and so did I, upon cloud nine with you around,
I forgot about my worries and everything that brought me down.
I spent every minute of each day with a ridiculous smile upon my face,
Everywhere I went, I kind of bounced around the place.
I never planned the time with you or all these years together,
I was so confused and lost I couldn't commit to anything never.
I never looked for love when I had held it so close to my heart,
And it had hurt me, made me cry, persisting to rip my world apart.
And although it may sound dramatic, I often can't believe my luck,
Meeting you like that was like being knocked down by a truck.
Like something so big was happening, I'd opened my eyes to see the truth,
A fool to keep on crying, wasting away my youth...
Now my days so different, replaced by the greatest of laughs and best of times,
A love I just deserved after all, for all my crimes.
I can't explain what you've done for me and what you still do, too much to tell
But upon finding love in your arms, it is true, I found myself as well.

Rachael Hewett

GOD'S VOWS TO ME

R: God, I'm ready
God: (shakes head and scoffs)

R: Lord I'm ready, steady and I'm going to find a man
Someone who loves me for everything that I am
A man who is after Your own heart
And is strong enough never to depart from Your Word
And he is going to be loving enough to shepherd Your herd
He'll be how like Jesus is to Your church
Trust me, I know what to avoid in this search
You see I've been there and done that
I've bought the T-shirt and sent it back
I'll never go out with a non-born-again, again

God: Again and again
You choose your will over Mine
And step out of the plans I have for you, which are divine
How many times are you going to walk down this *same* path
Every time you do this Satan just laughs
At you
If the victory is in Jesus what makes you think it's you
That can do everything yourself
When you still don't have a clue?
Your steps need to be ordered in
What My word tells you to do

R: Hold on a minute I don't think I understand
I've been reading Your Word, I know it like the back of my hand
I'm going to seek a husband
I'm going to wear that wedding band

Become the wife in Proverbs 31
Have children, that's the plan
I thought it was Yours too
You said it's better to marry than burn with lust and that's exactly
what I'm going to do
You said it's not good for man to be alone
Well same goes for women too
I have so much love to give in me
A love that's pure and true

God: I know it is, I put it there and that love is Me
But you give your love to everything else and never return it to Me
I've been so patient with you
Encouraging you to realise
That the only method that works
Stops you from having to compromise
Seek first My Kingdom and My righteousness
Make me your everything, so that I can bless
You with all things, and pass every test
You're a child of the King and so you deserve the best
And I am Your Creator and deserve nothing less

R: I'm so sorry and do apologise
Sometimes I get so caught up in myself and in the devil's lies
Not putting You first has led to my demise
It's Your will and commands that I should idealise
And You're gracious enough to bless me with a prize
When I'm following Your word to get me through this life
You deserve everything I have and more
How could I have brought someone into my life and kept You
behind a locked door

I'm so sorry

God: I know you are
Just seek Me first and My righteousness
And then all these things will be added onto you
You've been looking for fulfilment and love elsewhere
But here's something I've always had for you

I promise never to leave you nor forsake you
Because I'll always be here
Even if you forget how much I love and care
G: For you
R: And I
G: We have
R: Become
G & R: One

I'd give My life for you again and again
I sacrificed for you in love and through pain
Your body is My Spirit's temple which is the same
As saying you are My bride
And I will come back for you again

People will say I'm not really here for you
They'll also lie and say I'm not real
Your friends might try and introduce you to another
And might confuse the way you truly feel
But I need you to look deeper
So that I can reveal
That I am the cure for those friends who are ill

I need you to bear with me as I get jealous sometimes
But please understand it's because you're rightfully Mine

I cannot and will not share you with anything or anyone
I want to be your everything
Put higher above everyone

R: Lord I love You
I love You above and beyond everything I know
You are my true soul mate
You are everything I want and more
The best friend I could ever pray for
Only You can satisfy every one of my needs
And with every step that I take, I'll always let You lead
You've sacrificed so much for me
And I owe You everything
I want to grow so deep in You
That I'll forget about wanting 'that' ring

God: This is what I meant by My righteousness being added unto you
You won't have to seek a husband because he's going to find you
Keep on putting Me first
And all things will work out for your good
Cos I've loved you before time began when nobody else could.

RochelleLoRo

AN OCEAN BEYOND

I remember in London, the first time I saw you,
It was something special, I started to adore you,
The year was '07, I got into your room
There were so many people, you were great I assumed,
A glass screen in the middle, you were having your food,
I watched you laughing, it lifted my mood,
The last day in London, before you departed,
Unlocked a new chapter, one that had just started.

I sat in the crowd, as you walked past,
That magical spell, that you managed to cast (!)... over me.
I watched your last steps, and then you were gone,
I picked up some flowers you had just trodden on.
I put them in a bag, the moment was etched
Forever in my heart, so skillfully sketched.

I rang you one day, your sweet voice called my name,
Right then, you set fire to what was mere flame,
The fire which grew to denote our bond,
Words can't describe, what made me so fond,
I felt like a fish released from the pond
Of the material realm to an ocean beyond.

I really didn't know, quite what to say,
To He who controls dawn, dusk and day.
You spoke a few words, then the phone cut out,
My mum went mad, oh boy did she shout!
'Is that how you talk? Do you have any sense?'
But you weren't there to be in my defence.

I felt down, replaying our recorded conversation,
I went to my room, out of sheer frustration.
Soon fell asleep, and whilst I was sleeping,
You came in my dream and stopped me from weeping,
Sat down beside me, on my very bed
Your loving hand graced my undeserving head,
And made me feel like everything I'd said,
Meant the world to you...
...and that I shouldn't feel bad.
The next morning I woke up, no longer felt sad!

When we met again in India some years later,
I truly felt the presence of somebody greater
Than a mere mortal being, aged 90 in a wheelchair,
Your presence, say the scriptures, is incredibly rare,
Even for the gods, who long for human birth,
To catch a mere glimpse of your form on this Earth.

Then there was a long gap of two and a half years...
When I saw you after that long, there certainly were tears.
I forgot my own existence, waiting in the queue
For those forty-five minutes, twice a day, just to be with you.
When our eyes met one time, my mind completely froze.
Your loving gaze fell upon me, more tender than a rose.
You stared into my eyes, my past, future, present,
I felt waves and waves of bliss, so divinely pleasant,
I lost all notions of time when I sat with folded hands

But when I had to part my way, I didn't understand
What I had done to have to return to foreign-land,
The sound of the siren, before you'd come out,
Was all I really breathed for, how could I go without?

I cried, you know, when it was finally time to leave,
I couldn't say my byes and quietly I grieved,
I wasn't going anywhere until you came out again!
Running late for my flight, it was half-past ten...

I should've left an hour ago, as I desperately hoped
That you would come out once more, I clutched the last rope.
The clock struck eleven, I was just about to go,
When suddenly I turned, and you came to steal the show,
Alas... although
It was our last moment together.
You looked at me, I looked at you, it was over in a feather.

I quickly made my way, would I make it on time?
Apparently not, say the locals, not at this time
It's dark, dangerous, the journey will be slow,
If I didn't catch this flight, then only God knows...
What would've happened.
But in the end I made it there alright
I hopped on the plane and off went the flight
What's life if I can't forever be in your sight?
But our bond remains eternal, like a string to its kite.

Priyesh Patel

PERPLEXITIES OF LOVE

Love comes in numerous forms and guises
No particular feature and many sizes
A powerful emotion often difficult to control
With an unspecified motive and unknown role
Can lie dormant and only realised when lost
This devastation should be avoided at all cost
Some constantly search for the wonders once felt
Those feelings that consume and make one melt
Thought to be a drug by many, due to memories it can evoke
Being part of a magical dream from which you have just awoke
An inner warmth of contentment and wellbeing on meeting
Such a sensation has unbelievable force even if fleeting
When love is felt you are cocooned by an invisible cloak
You walk on air and constantly smile as if being told a funny joke
The intuitive understanding can astound and amaze at times
You can be confused and question the unspoken signs
Love's emotional reaction has such strength
That's why one's true love is sought at such great length
Some think love is a myth but still search none the less
Such is love's power or enigma I guess
The act of loving is within us all
Be receptive of kind gestures don't put up a wall
Love and be loved as you travel through the day
Who knows if your true love be near or far away
Each day is a new page of one's wonderful life
Fill it full of love and banish all strife.

Anne Sackey

TOGETHERNESS

We loved to be together in the
summer sun, again in the
evening when the day was done,
and we loved to walk along the
sandy beach to remove socks,
hose, tuck up trouser legs
and skirt, then to cool in the
sea those aching toes.

To be together when gathering
autumn fruits was always fun,
which was a reminder I did
this as a young boy for my dear
mum, quite a change from that
sandy beach but always found
the best fruit, of course, way out
of reach.

Together, we would search for
and collect the wild mushrooms
from the grass verges and the
local fields to be surprised,
sometimes at their more than
generous yield. Some were the
size of dinner plates,
unbelievably so, but there was
just that one field from which
to collect, if one knew where to go?

Our love we shared in the
springtime as we would walk
the country lanes, often to be
caught in sharp showers, then
rewarded by a glimpse of the
primrose, so beautiful, its
finest hour, displaying
its first flower.

At times we'd pause to listen
to the blackbird sing as he
perched on the old, five bar
gate, but off he would fly as
we approached, arriving just
that moment too late.

And that love we shared as we
walked gardens full of vibrant
colours which prompted us, as
we loved to do, just walk for
hours marvelling at the sheer
beauty of the azalea, this
amazing flower, and we'd watch
their reflection in the lakes, such
beauty to see, was always ours.

Those long, dark winter's eves
we shared music which touched
our hearts, performed by those
we had loved so much, right from
the start. We loved the artistry of
Sinatra, his interpretation of

each song, and Mozart's clarinet
concerto which went on and on,
and Ella Fitzgerald whose jazz
made one's toe tap, we loved her
songs. The big bands and the
musicals which we enjoyed so
much, and the Book At Bedtime
we would listen long to awaken
in the morning to find the story
long since gone.

And our love, our togetherness
brought us a son, our life had
changed, we had won but sadly,
he was to be the only one, with
so much love, so much fun, his
life, God bless him had just
begun.

We knew togetherness was
God-given and His to take away,
and so sadly my love was taken
from us one September day, but
I shall always love Iris Mary,
albeit, she is so far away.

Norman Lewis

PROMISING ETERNAL LOVE

'Will you marry me?' he shyly whispered,
'I'll put a ring on your finger,'
'Yes,' to him she gently whispered
Back - 'we mustn't linger.'

To the jewellers they hastily went
The selection in the shop window was vast
And they both knew a large amount of money would be spent
Their love for one another would forever last.

They selected a diamond ring set in white gold
It sparkled like the sunlight
And she knew she would wear it until she grew old
He was her ideal man - for him she was just right.

They would go to the ends of the world to declare their love
In church they would make their vows
Their words would rise to heaven above
And now in homage to one another each of them bows.

The world and life ahead of them would be filled with so much
Together they would weather both the storms and doldrums
They promised they would always go Dutch
And together work out all their sums.

They vowed too that nothing would ever split them up
To their dying day they promised and vowed their love
And would always be willing to drink from the same cup -
Their union would be blessed both here on earth and by heaven
above.

Patricia J Tausz

WITHOUT YOU

Without you I am nothing
A plaintiff voice rolling around inside an echo
Struggling to be heard
Like the mewing of a fledgling seabird
Abandoned on a cliff face edge
Before a desolate, chromium sea
With only my reflection haunting and taunting me.
Alone and swaddled in my chrysalis of fretting flesh
My wings crushed, my spirit broken,
My myriad words left unspoken;
A ghost unseen thro' the drifting haze
A witness to my own demise
Believing the lies I tell myself
With reality too hard to bear.
I would beg every passer-by passing there
For their reminiscences of you,
Fables, myths or anecdotes;
Has anyone any to spare?
Portraits I drew in my mind fast fading
Time washing them away;
Reverie mocking my febrile brain
Until I doubt your very existence.
Did you bend your gaze like light thro' a single raindrop
Splashing in my eye?
Your apparition burning with an intensity to blind.

Did we really stroll arms entwined
Lost in a world of our creation?
Whispering ear-to-ear that no one else should hear.

Taking fleeting moments to embrace,
To read each other's eyes;
To reflect the look of love
Stripped bare of all disguise.
Did we talk away the hours long into the night
With only shadows for company
Over wine by candlelight?

Weaving our tapestry of dreams
Of futuristic plans and schemes.
Did I sit hypnotised by your lilting voice?
Velvet over satin and silk;
Drizzling honey'd nectar over cream rich bee sting's milk.
And did we lie in our raw nakedness
Hidden from the spyglass moon?
Whilst Pan played pipes for you and me
As Eros called the tune,
For that most secret of moments
No witnesses should seek to see,
Like salt in the seas where the seals swim,
Like earth anchored roots of the trees
You are my need; my selfish greed.

All perfectly natural to me;
And when we part as one day we must,
One to return to the tail of stardust
Streaming from the cosmic wheel;
One to remain with the leftover life
To contemplate the sweetest deal
Known only to those who truly love;

Who surrender to that certainty
And for all eternity.

Philip J Mee

REMEMBER ME

Just because you can't see me, doesn't mean I've gone away.
I loved the life we shared together, and that love will always stay,
From the time you wake in the morning, until the close of every
day.
No matter where you are my darling, I'm never more than a
breath away.

I'm sad each time I see you cry, and it hurts to watch you grieve,
I wish I could prove to you that I'm near, so that you could truly
believe.
Then I think your sadness would be lifted a little and your life
would be easier to live.
If you can believe I'm here in spirit, then just think of the comfort
that I could give.

I smile with you when you smile, and I cry with you when you
weep.
I share your life through every day and I watch over you while you
sleep.
I treasured our life when I was here on Earth, you were my love,
my family, my friend
And that's the way it will always stay, until eternity comes to an
end.

So never feel you are all alone, that will never ever be.
Through the rest of your days on Earth my love, your guardian
angel will be me.
So always hold your head up high, and try not to grieve for what
used to be.
But keep our memories tucked safe in your heart, and smile when
you remember me.

Doreen Clarke

CUT MY HEART

You cut my heart wide open,
You smile there as you stand.
As the blood is pouring you stop to hold my hand.
I catch my breath.
As I hold my chest, I still don't understand.

I've lost my best friend.
What makes you think that is your reply.
The fact that you hurt me and constantly lie.
With that, I get no response just the silence of guilt.
The no eye contact, the no explanation why.

I can't find the words to say goodbye.
As I proceed to pack your belongings and question my heart.
Distracted by my brain as I start to cry.
I need you, I don't want you, I need you in my life.

I've gotten to the point where I realise it's a lie
I can no longer pretend.
As I constantly question my life.
You will never change and I don't understand why.

I've given you chance after chance.
You remain the same. Carry on like life's a game.
Don't let me stop you or get in your way.
I hope you look back and it all clicks one day.

But for now, I'll pack your stuff.
Push you out the door and wish you good luck.
Deep down I wanna try again, instead of going through all this
pain

How can I continue on the same hoping somehow things will change.

I could never see myself, ever being with anyone else.
But there you are again with your selfish ways.
So there is only one thing left to say.
Love is not enough to have you treat me this way.
So keep on walking I don't need you to explain.

You cut my heart wide open and stamped on it, as it fell to the floor.
You cut my heart wide open, and it no longer beats anymore.
You cut my heart wide open and stole it from my chest.
You cut my heart wide open, there still remains a space.
You cut my heart wide open and left an empty place.
You cut my heart wide open to find your intentions were cruel.
Now you've left me to deal with it all.

As you look on with my heart in your hands.
It doesn't really matter if I don't understand.
Just one more time will you hold my hand.
As I find the words to say goodbye.
I cannot help but cry.

Natasha Larmond

MY LOVE, MY LIFE

As sunset caresses a sandy beach with tendrils of evening,
Shades and hues of oranges and reds perfuse the sky,
Lengthening shadows complete the romantic vista.
A scene often set to depict love in all its glory.
Love has many stages, many types, many forms.
Is this how eternal love is seen to exist for all?
Indeed is there a definitive for eternal love?
Does it exist for real or is it something imagined?
Until we feel it for ourselves how do we know?
Feelings are so personal and totally individual,
The love I feel for my husband is unique to me.
I can't conceive that anyone else could feel such love.
I love him with every cell of my body, for always.
Is that eternal love? Is that what I am feeling?
Every day I wake, I stop and think of my fortune,
Riches incalculable way beyond any money.
A man who means so much to me, so very precious,
Who reciprocates in kind and feels as I do.
How fortunate am I to find this wonderful man?
So perfectly matched, we are so blessed, so happy.
Is this eternal love, does it last eternally?
Will we live forever if we find it, will our souls go on?
I can't imagine how I could feel more love for someone,
My heart already bursts with feelings for you,
You fill my thoughts each and every day,
I hate it when we are apart, even for an hour.
Time without you there is a waste of my life.
The only time worth spending is time with you.
You fill my every need, you are my soul mate,

Our minds as one interact freely through time,
We take as we give and live for each other,
In our own little world of happiness and contentment.
But do we have eternal love? I think we do.
How we define eternity is flexible. Our eternity.
That is our eternal love, as long as we are allowed
As long as the time we are allotted to spend with each other
Whether ten years, twelve, more, however many
That will be ours, our eternity of eternal love.
Our eternal love that we nurture every day
Every hour, every minute, every second, our Love.
We feel for each other now as always, total love.
From the day we met to the end of our eternal love.

Lynne Frodsham

SLOWLY LOSING MY MOTHER

I may never know how it feels to lose sight of all that is real
To forget what we remembered and remember what we knew
I can only offer an opinion
A very personal point of view

I felt pain like no other earlier today
When asked to introduce myself I heard my mother say
Of course I know who she is it's my sister I'm sure
But I was her first born, a daughter, she doesn't remember
anymore

This tale of loss isn't easy to begin
I stand on the outside helplessly looking in
It is only the sufferer that can attest to the frustration
Of memory loss experienced by an increasing part of the nation

The death of a parent is heart breaking
How do I describe losing a living breathing soul?
A person who thinks I am a visitor
A woman who no longer has goals

It is hard to watch this thief of life
As it nibbles viciously at her mind
Swallowing every vestige of sanity and joy
Removing thoughts of her girl and her four boys

Most of us fret when we lose a key or our phone
Imagine not knowing your way back home
My dad is her carer and a very proud man
With minimum assistance he does the best that he can

This time on earth is so fleeting
Many beautiful things complete our lives
Pain has carved a place on the face of my father
At the slow disappearance of his wife

So I mourn whilst the life is still living
Day after day I watch as the changes occur
I hope for a miracle and return to normality
Not for me you understand but for her

There are occasional periods of lucidity
When the hurt and confusion shines bright in her eyes
But no matter how arduous the journey
I will never move far from her side

For this is the person who ensured my safety
Gave me guidance in times of stress and pain
The least I can do for my parents
Is offering them both the same.

Lynn Noone

GOODBYE

Don't you remember,
The lengths you went to,
Trying to woo,
Confessing your heart,
To not let us part.
Stroking my face,
Slow is our pace,
Liking how our lips taste.
Ten million stars,
Forgetting ten million scars,
Only bright lights of the moon,
Outlined my body as you swooned.
Singing aloud in your car,
Driving so very far,
To just be together,
Elating as quick as a feather.
Telling me to have no tears,
About who I am,
As to have those fears,
Contradicts his own ideas.
Sat with your mother,
With wide smiles and laughter,
About your incapability,
To face life with bear-ability.
As we watched a movie,
You looked at me with the idea,
Of where we were was nothing but beauty.
From friendship to relationship,
You kissed my lips,

Rosy cheeked with cold fingertips,
You warmed my breath,
Like Romeo and Juliet.
Out of the blue,
Not giving me a clue,
My phone went silent,
Despite what I sent.
Summer days,
You forced a distance,
Large enough for your stunts,
And like a fool I clung.
You said, 'I never meant to lead you on,'
Your word meant nothing,
To you it was a fling,
Of trying new things,
To forget your heartache,
You played me like a king.
But to rekindle our friendship,
You thought you could flick a switch,
So I stayed strong,
To remain like the one who won,
In a tragic love song.
Yet again you let me down,
For you didn't make a sound,
Leaving me in the dark,
For months went by,
Without a single note of goodbye.
Now I have changed,
My self-image and ways,
Leaving you behind,

My life I have re-arranged.
But that was one time,
In a small town with one guy,
Whose rhyme I left behind,
For now it's too late,
Once you say goodbye,
I do not wait.

Megan Dodson

WINTER WIDOWER

Harsh awakenings, cold and lonesome now that she has gone
Where is purpose? Where is joy? All comforts remain but nothing

The warming aroma of coffee to wake the senses, the peaceful
song of the morning birds amongst the rising glow of a new day
How wonderful! I exclaim, a silent call

A walk in the bright brisk winter morn
Silver frost layering the fields
No skin to touch, both hands and heart longing
Much colder these walks now without your smile
The wooden bench, our secret escape to rest, to think, to talk, to
be silent, to be together, our place, only you, only me
My own now but far more special shared
Let me sit for a while, let me take in the view across the fields

I miss you more with each passing breath that enters the winter
air
My heart broken and forever in love
Let me sit for a while, let me rest, let me close my tired eyes
I long for you my dear as my breath shortens in the winter freeze
but I'm no longer cold, no longer scared

My heart is mending as darkness draws, I will be with you now,
God has heard my call
Light fills my soul as I feel your touch, time to awake with you
again
Together at last.

Dan Black

BUILDER'S MATE

He approached me directly
Assessing - estimating with his eyes,
Weighing the cost of this approach against
The possible profit.
Would I be worth the prize?

He liked the way I looked.
No subsidence in my walk
More to me than window dressing,
No sign of cosmetic cover-up in my talk.

I noted...
Rough hands, painted clothes but,
Uncovered a smooth heart.
Confident, competent, clear minded and consistent.

This builder, took his time
No bish bash bosh... or ball of demolition.
Knowing that 'Rome wasn't built in a day'
That a firm foundation is *the only* way.

Gradually, his warmth's radiated through me.
He's carpeted me with wall to wall affection,
Seen me stripped back to the core,
Brought only support no less, no more.
Never expecting me to be someone else,
No pretence...
He knows the score.

As years passed, around me he's built a scaffold of love,
Plastered over my faults and cracks

With hopefulness.
Replacing the windows to my resistance
By his honesty and persistence
With a new vista.

Choosing only
To see my investment potential.

Of course,
At times there have been sparks of anger and delight,
We've chiselled at these until we took flight.
Dismantled each issue... stone by stone...
We prefer life together
Not alone.
Brick by brick a relationship made
Soldered with trust, love and respect
No facade.

I'm so happy I said 'yes' to that first date
And my life makeover.
13 years and, still building a friendship.
Cementing our happiness
No conventional
Structure to our relationship
Still... It's
A Grand Design.

Laura Annansingh

NOT NOW, NOT TODAY

I am here, I'm holding your hand, it's time, to say goodbye,
I don't need words, for you know me, and how this feels.
Do you remember, we were so young once, with no reason to cry,
and we had wings upon our heels.

I loved you too much for it to end like this,
but knew, some time, life would turn this way,
So I am prepared to say goodbye, with a final kiss,
but please, just not now, please; not today.

We vowed in God and lived in love,
and we wove our lives together.
We scaled the heights and touched God's face,
believing it would be this way forever.

I loved you too much, for it to end like this,
and now, life has turned this way,
I will only get just one chance, for our final kiss
please God, help me, it's now, today.

I don't regret a single day that the sun rose on our life,
but now, my heart is just broken, and sore.
To think, the last sun has risen on the life we will share,
I'd trade the rest of mine for just one day more.

I loved you too much for it to end like this
and now life is in the way.
Tears fall from me, all grace departs, I placed my final kiss.
My heart, my love died, today.

The first sun rose this morning, on a world you and I no longer share,
I cried all night, dreams of you youthful, again, my own.
Then I woke and remembered, oh the aching, God, the wound,
this is the first day, this is life, I'm alone.

I loved you too much for it to end like this,
and grief tears and bears down on me it's true.
I will honour you by smiling and loving life as we did,
Until life turns again, and returns me to you.

Barry Mullan

ETERNALLY ORPHIC LOVE

Caress me with your wisdom
Fill me with your mind
Penetrate my deepest thoughts
And let our souls entwine.

Kiss my inspirations
Ruffle through my sins
Delve into my very core
And underneath my skin.

Behold more than my beauty
Desire more than my shape
Yearn to know my secrets
And let none of them escape.

Read more than my cover
Touch more than just my spine
Drink up every chapter
And thirst for every line.

Ache to touch my psyche
Long before you touch my heart
Crave to taste my character
And all its hidden parts.

Hunger for my story
And not just my physique
Show me that my number
Ain't the *only* thing you seek.

Arouse me with your intellect
And move me with your words

Tease me with philosophy
And leave me undeterred.

Touch me with your naked thoughts
And woo me with some *zest!*
A man with some intelligence
Is hotter to undress.

Long to share my wildest dreams
And anchor my devotion
Revel in life's mysteries
Express your raw emotions.

Impress me with perception
And speak with true intent
Challenge my opinions
But always be a gent.

Adore imagination
Conversations, dearly treasure
And I'll gladly give my heart and soul
To you, in equal measure.

Accept my insecurities
And shake my darkest fears
Show me only kindness
And love, beyond our years.

So let me bare my soul with you
And let our worlds collide
Share with me eternal love
That knows, no place, to hide.

Kelly Hurst

LOVED ONES

Dearest Garden,
You have my eternal love
And a pocket full of childhood memories
The thought of inhaling breaths of the most intoxicating
fragrances
Spinning with bouquet in hand until blue skies turned to fairy floss
Anticipating that crisp first bite of hand-picked fruit
Like a patchwork quilt with a border of green grass
It was home to small creatures and sweet love songs
Echoing through the trees
Shade from summer's heat
Spiderwebs networking industriously through the beds
Butterflies chasing my bouncing curly locks as I ran through the
maze of vines and climbers
Grandma gathered a harvest within her gingham apron folds
Together we'd parade to the kitchen for baked scones and jam
I marvel now
For at my fingertips was an expression of a lifelong passion
An endless love for me

Dear Sons
You have our eternal love
From the very moment you were born (six minutes apart)
The sweetness of your delicate skin and tiny fingers and toes
Twice blessed all at once
You came to know the beauty of food
Harvested from our very garden
Meals fashioned in your father's kitchen
Learning the basics as you watched intently from your highchairs

You also grew to hunger for stories, music, games and family conversations
We encouraged your openness to travel
Nurtured your curiosities
A world filled with possibilities
School, university, careers
Every moment precious
Now separated by distant shores we long to be together once more
At times we shed tears of pride, hope and anticipation
For at the very core of our beings is an expression of a lifelong passion
An endless love for you

Geraldine Marcellino

THE 15TH ARCHER

As I exhale, mist condensates prudently on the mirror.
I tentatively write down what my mind won't comprehend, 'Love'.
Gradually the mist evaporates, and the world I hesitantly wrote
down vanishes.
I inhale deeply, with the hope of breathing in new life to melt the
ice crevice around my heart,
Deeply embedded in my thoughts, there was no reason to seek
change.
My mind confined to a box of self-pleasure. Reclusively
unapologetic.
I knew no better. Like a crab, crawling in and out of my shell as
the rain constantly overshadowed the rainbows.
Insensitive?
Maybe somewhat.
I blame it on the unfulfilled promises that led to the cold shackles
around my mind, which imprisoned my body and held my heart
hostage.
Yet still hoping to be released from obscurity, the diminished fire
within me ignited.
The warmth transmitting hope into my veins, awakening new life.
Just like the subtle moment the caterpillar emerges from its
cocoon.
Until one day, a ray of light beams in my face, and your radiance
illuminates my body.
In your presence; butterflies swamp my insides, as they float and
reside deep where it's most secretive.

I look at you in awe, and simply stay silent.
Taking in your energy as it fuels my desire to make you the one
and only.

I hold your face as I kiss you.
Simultaneously closing our eyes as we drift into cloud nine.
Soaring high as we overlook the horizon at sunrise.
Bodies entwine gracefully as we share an intimate moment.
Heartbeats synchronising to one beat as our cohesiveness is
unmatched.
Your warmth has melted the ice block within.
I exhale, and the mist is no more.

Melvin Uwaibi

THE WOUNDER'S WHIP

The heart hears his words,
Drenched with a laboured longing,
The cries of the vulnerable, naked,
Detached from the body
You slapped me alive.

You were the owl's song in the veil of night,
The impossible equation I could not solve,
The compass point I could not follow,
The truth of my smile.

I would hate you if I did not love you.
The wounded whip lies at the foot of my bed,
Where I and our clothes fell,
Where the carpet curls around your footprints.

The door waits to open on our sins and lies,
Where I stand, where I stood, where I lay.
Time has coated the champagne cork in dust,
It rolled under the bed the day you left.

You were the endless night of stars,
The lover's tongue that tasted eternal,
The dare in my dreams,
The hunger in my stare.

I drift through the drudge of the day,
See your face in the camera's mirror,
And want to tear your image out and make you real,
Tear you like paper, a dictionary for despair.

In your world, you pour coffee and share its heat with someone else.
In your world, our door is closed, the cellar of secrets sealed shut.
In your world of husband, father, son, brother, you give rope for the women to bind you.
I would lend them my whip, but it's wounded and thick with the blood of me and has lost its lash.
I can smell you on its leathered grip.

You were the sea that I could not sail,
The promise that could not be delivered,
The risen from the ruin,
The husband of a woman you call wife.

Dawn Bradley

I WANT YOU TO FEEL LOVE

This loss of love, the loss of us,
I want you to understand this,
I need you to understand this,
I hope that you understand this.

If you don't know love,
If you don't understand love,
If you don't experience love,
You cannot love or be loved.

Is it my role to show you love?
Is it my role to teach you about love?
Is it my role to help you to feel love?
Is it my role to give you love?

I want you to know love,
I want you to feel love,
I want you to know my love,
I want you to feel my love.

This loss of love, the loss of us,
I want you to feel this,
I need you to feel this,
I hope that you feel this.

If you don't know this love,
If you don't feel this love,
If you don't experience this love,
You cannot love or be loved.

What makes you scared of love?
What makes you fear feeling loved?

What makes you fear giving love?
What makes you fear being in love?

I don't want you to be scared by love,
I don't want you to fear feeling love,
I don't want you to fear giving love,
I don't want you to fear being in love.

You are safe to know love with me,
You are safe to feel love with me,
You are safe to receive my love,
You are safe to be in love with me.

If you don't feel the loss of this love,
If you don't understand the loss of this love,
Feel the loss of me,
Understand the loss of me,
That is the loss of love.
You do feel love.

Allison Hanbury

AT FIRST SIGHT

Well, Valentine's Day was miles away,
Summertime was coming to an end.
Yet that blonde was up for a love game.
As if he'd had a crush on me, he was chasing me like mad,
Was dancing in the streets in his black cab.
So obsessed, he was dicing with death.
Nothing spectacular I had on, not even a red hat
Just a brown leather jacket and a yellow skirt.
Though I was heading home, now I had to change direction,
From this awkward situation I planned an escape,
Walked fast, almost ran in exasperation.
Behind the roundabout and bridge I felt quite safe.
It was there, where he caught up with me to my consternation.
We were face-to-face, I found he was taller than myself.
Before I knew what to expect, he grabbed my hand
And dragged me to the other side of the road,
Where his car was waiting, first
He offered me a drink at the nearby pub
When I refused he opened the door of his cab
And invited me inside.
As I declined once more, dejected he sped off.
The next day, still at a loss and trying to cope,
About the incident to the acquaintance I spoke.
She made me more stunned by excitement she failed to hide
'Wow!' she exclaimed. 'You should have taken the plunge.
That was love at first sight
For you the guy was risking his life!'
I still can't decide if she wanted to make me laugh
Or blow off my mind.

Do you think she wasn't smart enough
To tell a fake from a true love that lasts?
What was the case? As my prince did he qualify?

Lucy Carrington

EMPIRE

I have my own world, where I've built you an Empire.
And in this Empire are many wondrous items.
There are performers and artists, who never tire,
And mythical beasts from Greek stories of Titans.

There is rhubarb and honey, gifts from plants and bees,
Coupled together with placid lakes and plush trees,
Where their leaves reach out into emerald green seas,
So temperate, we shall not heat, nor shall we freeze.

And in this Empire there are the sounds of fiction,
Amplified by the raw beauty of the landscape.
These have come to being through my own creation
In this land where our minds can together escape.

And in this Empire there is the perfect lagoon
That holds the reflection of the clearest full moon.
White sand beaches, where one dreams of falling maroon
And we lie there together in eternal noon.

As the grand night draws in after our timeless day,
We retire to the castle with drawbridge and moat,
Where the feast is set in Parisian cafés
And dessert is offshore, on a luxury boat.

We go hand in hand, off the boat onto firm land
Where between our toes there is green grass and warm sand.
Ahead in the marquee is a four-piece string band,
Whose music we waltz; then together we stand.

As I pull you close to press my lips against yours.
Your soft silk skin, so precious as I hold you tight.
With only us and the calm starry night outdoors
Watching our eternal love forever shine bright.

Alex Roberts

THE PRETTY PEACH

I'm not taking the piss
But it was just a kiss
As much of a cliché as this is
It all started as a misfit, it was just business
We weren't fit for each other
As the only fit definition that we would mention is the aesthetics
of one another

But we bravely jumped in feet first
Though we were warned that we'd just get hurt
We feigned ignorance
Yet the brilliance that broke our defence made it different
You said you wanted to keep your distance
Broke it off and took off within an instant

We were scared
So unprepared to lay bare things undeclared
Feelings were getting in the way
And we ignored what people had to say
To us it was just drunk sex, so what did we expect?
For things to just fizzle away?

No surprise, it didn't
We both left a little imprint
A little something that would grow within an instant
And it scared me
I'm just an idiot paired with someone clumsy
Like a strange fantasy or superhero comedy

I'm rambling
What I'm trying to say, see
Is that lately I've been debating why I've been questioning what's
in front of me
Cos it ain't science or mystery, it's just blatantly
You and me enjoying each other's company
And there's no shame in it

But this ain't a bloody motivational speech
I'm just inspired by the desire to admire that pretty - uh - peach
Or bum, so to speak.

Gk Kearse

FATEFUL VOYAGE THROUGH ETERNITY

Made for each other
Two kindred souls unite
Ordained at birth
And fated to meet
Heart and spirit merge
To make one complete

As one

Being of same thought spirit and mind
Friendship firmly rooted in firm ground
Hearts permanently entwined
A spark ignited the eternal fire
From a single heavenly kiss
And magic tender moments of euphoric bliss

Travelling through life's hills and vale
True love a journey only two know and sail
On warm temperate waves of emotion.

Beauty abounds with caring, sharing and giving
Bonds growing stronger in the glorious summer
Of blissful living
Every day a new fragrant flower grows
With every loving kiss bestowed
On lips made to fit
And awakening tender teasing fingertips.

Sanctuary found in each other's comforting arms
An oasis in a desert free from harm, full of grace and charm
A special kind of love that few have found
Seeds of love grown in fertile ground
The reason to be
The most precious gift of all
companion through life
A loving husband and loving wife.

As winter arrives

The roses still bloom
With their heady sweet perfume
Their love survives
One flesh until death
And beyond

The flame passed on to
Their children
And their children
And on

And on.

For eternity.

Peter Dome

LONG WAY BACK

'I cry freedom', was no answer,
It just didn't 'Make my day'.
Falling more into the chasm,
Took the future clean away.

Like the day with no tomorrow,
Like the seasons out of tune.
Like a mountain with no summit,
Like a road where darkness loomed.

I just didn't see it coming,
As it hit me, low and fast.
And so reaching for a lifeline,
I look deep into the past.
But nothing comes to save me,
So then will I, breathe my last...

Looking for a calmer highway
As I wander far and wide.
Could there be a new direction,
Still without you by my side...

Like the day with no tomorrow,
Like the seasons out of tune.
Like a mountain with no summit,
Like a road where darkness loomed.

Is that a glimmer of redemption,
I see coming round the bend.
Or just another sad, false prophet,
That the devil often sends...

Like the day you don't remember,
Like the silent drive back home
Like the sound of shallow breathing,
As I plead upon the phone...

If you see me heading your way,
You should take another road.
As I may just drag you under,
For I cannot bear this load...

Will I ever reach tomorrow,
Will the seasons come too soon.
Will the mountains start to plummet,
Will the road 'Engulf the fool...'

Sheffphil

1216

The winter days are breaking
And the mist is creeping in
Although the air is colder now
I'm happier within

When all around is joyful
It's harder to be sad
With frosty gems that furnish stems
When earth is icy clad

The chilled air brings a warmth within
Jack Frost offers his hand
He leads me through familiar routes
That feel like foreign land

Frosty dancers leap up high
Touching every tree
A dewy blanket glistens
And a robin looks at me

He stops, I stare, he doesn't move
His breast matches my nose
A loved one watching over me
Is how the saying goes

I don't believe in heaven
Yet I think I know this bird
His eyes, I've met this soul before
His song is one I've heard

A minute nearly passes now
And neither being moved
He wants me to acknowledge him
He wants his presence proved

A sharp intake of icy breath
I look at him and say
'I know you see me little bird
Please know that I'm OK'

He nods his beak, with one last glance
A ruffle, and he's flown
I watch him getting smaller
Till I'm sure that he is gone

See winter brings us magic
That not everyone can see
But I for one will not forget
The robin's gaze at me.

Lucy Willett

THE ROCK IN MY HEART'S SOFT SPOT

Carefree in the arms of my cornerstone
Anywhere in this world is my comfort zone
And the memories we share and call our own
Warm my bones when it's cold and I'm alone.

Your feather-light touch still melts my heart
Even when our hands are worlds apart,
Because, you are the rock in my heart's soft spot
And without you I only see what I'm not...

Life seems so hollow without you,
Tomorrow promises nothing new
And all the dreams I used to pursue
Seem to have no meaning and no value.

So, it's the thought of you I hold on to
When the bottom of my world falls through,
Because, only you can come to my rescue,
Stop me falling and make dreams come true.

And with every breath of mine that you take
The depths of my soul you stir and wake,
But just one tear, is all it takes to break
The spirit and heart of the man you could make.

You can expose every weakness I disguise
Leave me speechless as I close my eyes,
Because, it's your kiss that supplies
Rainbows in my lows and butterflies in my highs.

So until there is nothing left but death
I'll fight for your kiss to take my last breath,
And every smile you wear I will die to defend
Until the falling sky brings this world to an end.

Stuart Brisco

BREAKING UP

If he left her with a promise

Meaning forever
meant to be lifelong
love
or bliss
or rapture

Or whatever
makes for
eternal joy

Is that
a naive
Persuasion?
Or a constancy?

Suppose
a child may believe
in love's perfections

Or fidelities

as if a person
is as faithful
as a loved pet

Or a saint

Or a kiss

Or a calendar date

But love is not ideal
It shatters and is fragile
Like a broken china mug
Only still intact
in eyes of
the beguiled beholder
whose eyes weep real tears
not crocodile ones

Or blink

Or become misled
and hoodwinked
and disappointed

So no love ever lasts
forever

Since no one is perfect

Unless we lie
making a mirage of love
disguising lies and falsities

When love is no love at all
only an aspiration
which we fail to fulfil

For there is no heaven on earth
only human fallibility
which cracks, like a smashed mirror
into atoms, or a nothingness...

Which is sad
But probably
So very true...

Tracy Allott

ALAINA MAI COTTRELL

Something wasn't right and deep down I knew
Too scared to do what needed to be done, I had to be strong
The courage came and the magic moment arrived
Such joy rushing through my veins, lighting up my world

The first flutter made my heart skip a beat
Eagerly counting down the milestones with fascination
Excitement pouring out of every part of my body
The anticipation of the day you were due piercing my soul

All of a sudden the time had arrived to meet my little girl
The second you entered the world my life changed forever
I looked down at you and saw a vision of pure beauty
With an instant rush of love like no other will know

For two weeks now I have watched you grow
You become more perfect with every passing day
Your eyes are so alert looking at all the wondrous new sights
With a smile that could warm the coldest realms

My heart is on fire burning with unconditional love for you
I feel our bond already, so indestructible growing stronger day by day
Thank you my darling for making our family complete
My perfect pure and beautiful baby Alaina Mai

Kayleigh Cottrell

THE OLD SOLDIER

He didn't have long, his body said so
As he turned the dial on his old radio
News of a war in faraway lands
The memories came back
He started wringing his hands

He remembered it all, this killing game
The leaders have changed, but the price is the same
Young fresh faces marching to war
His sigh was deep, he'd seen it before

He cast a weary eye, on a well worn path
Today's victory is tomorrow's cenotaph
The sounds of war chilled him to the bone
He was one of the few who had made it home

They'd all get together every November
A wreath of poppies, they would always remember
There once was many, but now so few
His brothers in arms, only they really knew

His wife had passed, his children had flown
It was eight years now in this nursing home
Good friends he'd made, many had passed
He knew deep down that this day was his last

The final sleep he held no fear
He would meet them again all he held dear
Uniform on, medals on his chest
He lay on his bed for his final rest

The radio played her favourite song
His eyes grew heavy, it wouldn't be long
The years well spent, sleep peacefully came
His wife was there, she was calling his name.

John Astley

IN THE LAUNDROMAT, WASHING THE SHORTS OF THE MAN YOU LOVE

They stand alone, moulded in his image -
white skin transplanted to a washing machine.
They need soap and stronger seams.
Oh cheek covers, like leaves in a book fluttering
at the suggestion of an erotic scene!
They are a favourite story, a recurring episode
in the art of daily living and surviving trivia.
They hibernate in the laundry basket,
sheltering under shirts,
cowering when he scanned the empty drawer,
needing them the way you wait for eggs to boil.

Laundry day equals coronation of the queen.
There's a heraldry of water and washing machines;
his dirt spins round, there is a feast of gobbled coins.
Then comes the thought of that inner layer, now clean,
resting against his male flesh and outer cloth the world sees.
They tumble out, pristine, hot and innocent,
soft as a puppy between the towels.
They fold meekly, his manhood compliant in my hands.

Oh underwear, how vulnerable you seem!
His hidden garb aired in this public room with implied trust
to be discreet; not to caress them, just bring them home
in a sweet warm load of clean attire,

and say nothing of the ritual, the lingering touch,
the love that pervades such simple things -
the handling of your lover's dirty clothes.

Karen Eberhardt-Shelton

THRU

For you
I will cross the glass to bring back hope
For you
I'll deny time flows but all I'll cope
For you
I can't change the past or what's amid
For you
I will say I'm sorry for what I did

Gripping set of questions
Challenging the order
Attachment, possessions
Am I just a warder?

Mad is what they call me
As I'm never sure you're here
But I know they don't see
We lack a puppeteer

For you
I will cross the glass to bring back hope
For you
I'll deny time flows but all I'll cope
For you
I can't change the past or what's amid
For you
I will say I'm sorry for what I did

Cherishing the moment
Never seemed enough for me
I am no exponent
But still hope you'll disagree

Beating pawns is easy
Feel I'm shrinking by your side
But the mirror's queasy
Thru flaky world I will ride

For you....

Humpty Dumpty sat on a wall
Humpty Dumpty lowly and small
Only your favour in all kinds of weather
Can bring Humpty Dumpty together...

Agnieszka Majcher

IT MAY NOT ALWAYS BE SO

Dedicated to my wonderful husband, Cyril

It may not always be so
That we spend all our days at ease
Sampling the delights of summer and winter
When you would bring me the first sweetpeas
From the garden, with a secret smile.
We would sit in the summer house
And drink our tea and doze for a while
Our contentment complete.

It may not always be so
That we could gaze far out to sea
From the window of our holiday hotel
Strolling along the prom in the twilight
Of a warm summer's evening
Holding hands - no need for words
The quiet murmur of waves lapping the shore
A little paradise on Earth.

It may not always be so
These days of roses and wine
Each day a blessing and a gift.
Days out at stately homes to dine
A concert or perhaps a theatre trip.
These golden times of our later years.
We give thanks for all the abundance
And, for a while forget our fears.

The day will come when we have to part
One of us going on ahead to glory.

The tears will flow from the very heart
but that will not be the end of the story.
Love is eternal and memories are forever.
One day we shall meet again -
Home at last - no one will sever
The story of our love for each other.

June Smith

I WANT YOU

I fed you, clothed you
Kept you warm
I kept you safe from the day you were born

I tried to protect you
The best that I could
I love you in every way
Just like a mother should

The world is a bad place
I want to wrap you up in cotton wool
Keep you away from the bad things in life
And everything else that is cruel

I can't wrap you up or
Protect you forever
I want you to make mistakes
And learn it's better to be a giver

I want you to be happy
With confidence in all you do
I want you to believe in yourself
The way that I believe in you

I want you to grow up
Be popular and be yourself
I want you to follow your dreams
And live in perfect health

I want your knight in shining armour
To knock you off your feet
To love you faithfully forever
And be what makes his heart beat

I want you to know that
No matter what life throws your way
Unconditionally I'll always love you
Even after my dying day

Even then I will be your angel
Try to guard you from the bad
For now I'll be your best friend,
Your confidant, you mum and dad.

Julie Murphy

KISS THE TWILIGHT

What breathless tremors must I suffer
Through the night,
What remedy will assuage the heartache
I must endure,
Now that you are gone,
How can I live through the dark shadows
Of emptiness,
Blind to the scent of woodland
And verdant pastures
Where once we walked,
Hands intertwined, inseparable.

Our troubles and joys
Shared over the years
Promises made,
Now distant memories,
I should have loved you more,
Should have held you more,
But you were always there
Indelibly etched in my life.

Things left unsaid,
Haunt me in the night,
Hours and days wasted
In fruitless silences,
But you were always with me.

I wander aimlessly
Tied by the shackles
Of loneliness
Binding and smothering.

Without you I seek refuge and solace
Where the sun reigns in golden splendour,
Where the breeze is warm,
And the shadows of twilight
Remind me the day is dying.

Without you my torment
Removes the will to live,
Let me go down with the sun,
Let me say goodnight
To me festering grief,
Let me kiss the twilight.

Richard Kinsella

OUR LOVE

My love is like the morning dew
That hangs as tears on the waking bloom,
My love reached out its arms to you,
Revealing the door to that secret room,
And if certain loves are like the red rose,
My love is a flower that constantly grows.

Your love is like a sprouting tree
That bursts and craves to touch the sky,
Your love appeared and clung fast to me,
Leaving scarce choice but to join it and fly,
And if there are loves sweeter than any God's nectar,
Your love is the sweetest and the purest by far.

Our love is like an unchartered ocean
That stretches unhindered from shore to shore,
Our love exploded and set the stars in motion,
Spreading the divine music no one can ignore,
And if any love might be captured and measured,
Our love would be the outlaw, envied and treasured.

My love is like an evening prayer
That soars in gladness as the light fades,
My love grew wings and helped us share
The mystery and magic of those silent glades,
And if you still wonder if my love will remain true,
The red rose that my heart is beats uniquely for you.

Peter Dietrich

LOVE?

'Love' has no meaning
'Love' has no soul
Simply a word
with a rotating role...

Love is just a word we use to describe all and sundry
'Love you' 'hate you' can seem to make it all sound grungy.
Love is an intricate word heard time and time again.
Descriptive in so many ways to cause a lot of pain...

Love is just a word to use as and when it's needed.
'Love that dress,' 'love those shoes,' recognised, not heeded...
'Love to come and visit you' said through gritted teeth,
'Give my love to Arthur', as you quietly seethe...

'Love' in games means nothing, nil... 'loves' to find mistakes,
'No love lost between them', 'love lies bleeding as you rake'
I just 'love' to be poetic, 'love' is in such constant use
Does not make it any better, 'love' to me is just a ruse...

'Love' is an expressive word but when all is said and done
'Love' to me is just a word that creates a right good pun...

'Love?'

Charles Henry

INK

Ink:
it settles on a page,
lingering and kissing paper;
it seeps and caresses fabric of bark and leaf.
Over time,
after smudges and rips,
with folds and dogs' ears,
it fades

to a subtler ink
(a lesser blue or gentler black)
but stays, somewhere,
there,
still. Kept. Known.

Memory:
the erasable ink of schoolchildren's pencil cases,
the invisible ink of unsolvable clues;
it succumbs to a flame as paper
curls under head and
twists within cinder.

It cannot be annotated;
neither bookmarked nor copied.

What is library without book?
What is pen without ink?
What is mind without memory?

What, then, is heart without love?

Imagine:
a bookcase with gaps along shelves
and see teeth smacked out of a mouth.
Then, picture a decaying mind like
dyed saliva from a pen's lip:
going, losing, waning, discolouring...
but trying, willing, wanting

to stay and be read
to be loved

still

Thomas Harrison

SHE WAS ALWAYS THERE

She's sitting in the twilight,
Just rocking in her chair;
The house was very silent,
No other person there.

Her life, it was quite lonely,
No relative or friend.
Just me, the child she'd taken to,
On her I could depend.

She always took great care of me,
I loved her all the while.
She'd calm my fears and wipe my tears;
Until she saw me smile.

The treasures that belonged to us;
Well, money couldn't buy.
A happy home, a loving mum,
Without them I would die.

It always was so comforting;
In the firelight's glow;
Toasting crumpets on a fork,
Outside, was falling snow.

The Count of Monte Cristo
On the radio,
Sitting in the darkness,
Just the firelight's glow.

Very few possessions,
Nothing left to spare,
Mum's life, it was very hard.
It always seemed unfair.

Always I'll remember;
Those days of long ago,
And how I'll keep Mum in my heart,
Because I loved her so.

Beryl Heathcote

LET DOWN

What have I been doing that's so wrong?
Help me someone, tell me what is going on.
I thought that he loved me, I am so hurt inside.
I have just found out he thinks the grass is greener on the other side.

How trusting I have been, so loving and caring
I did not know that I had been sharing him with another.
I have found out now, she has blown his cover.

She phoned me to say they are having an affair, my heart hit the floor
My whole body shaking, I slumped against the door.
I tried to say something but no sound would come.
My whole being went numb.

Shall I confront him or just keep silent?
What shall I do, my mind is in torment
I did confront him and instead of a denial
He said, 'Yes, it is true let's have a separation, say two months trial.'

I looked around at the little house I loved so much
The garden that everyone said had the Midas touch

A silent goodbye as I closed the front door.

There is no eternal love for me here anymore.

Sylvia Papier

WHEN LOVE BEGINS

When love begins, the world around becomes a safer place,
Every trouble disappears, with a warm embrace.

When love begins, the mind is filled, with delightful thoughts,
And all at once, the life you know, is seemingly too short.

When love begins, a change occurs, you never could foresee,
Which makes you feel as wonderful, as you could ever be.

When love begins, a beaming smile, appears from ear to ear,
And laughter is the only thing, that comes before a tear.

When love endures, its radiance grows deep within the heart,
Each moment is more beautiful, than when you were apart.

When love endures, a gentle touch can tell a thousand words,
And time before your paths were crossed, is gradually blurred.

When love endures, the days are met, with a sense of bliss,
For you have met the person, who can save you with a kiss.

When love endures, you'll lead a never-ending romance plot,
What better way to celebrate, than to tie the knot?

Maria Kekic

INDEPENDENCE DAY

Blustery and grey,
Winter charm,
Nowhere to be seen,
Covered in leaves,
On the grass and in our tea,
Lit up by the blonde light,

Pretty as can be,
How can today happen,
With nothing more,
One step forward,
Two steps back,

Everything and thank you,
We professed about,
Over a mile or two,
With cups of brew,

Laugh and sigh,
Bump and divide,
Common ground,
Shared all around,

Is it okay to feel,
That it just isn't enough,
Saying goodbye,
Left with a number,

Can I trust to not lust,
With this number,
Delete or repeat,
Past mistakes,

Is this closure?
It feels so opaque,
A prism of anxiety,
More complex than ever,
She's had time to think,
Still no sign of a chink,
Questions bear the marks,
Of years gone past,
Go for it or,
Let it be,

In the end she leaves
To see and breathe
The life of this bear
So unplanned and free.

Adam Soliman

LOVE IS A CAGE

Metaphors aren't real
They force reality into something
Greater and deeper, unlike love
A simile: as good as it gets
An ever changing illusion.
Enthralled in a book-like scenario
Romance is just a genre
An echoing tap you can't tighten
Dripping into your bones
His poison you must have more of.
Wing tips cut while your dreamy gaze
Rests in his left palm
You're loyal like a dog
How you bark and won't bite
Now he sees a dog
Yet you swoon and bay
No cage necessary
For you have no wings
No longer is he a gentleman
No longer a gardener and
You accept, folding into yourself
Defeated
Metaphorically speaking, you say:
'I'm a fallen angel'
Simile:
'You're like a fallen angel'
'Love is like a cage, bars
Made out of brittle filigree
Ideological death of loneliness

And the ease of sating desire
It is a nostrum
And a palimpsest'
There is no cage
You can fly away.

Neth Brown

LOVE

I was once a jam jar
but contained within me
are all the things, you cannot see
to keep a happy family,

There's trust and kindness
and a whole heap of passion
the kind you'll find
won't go out of fashion,

There's patience and understanding
for when times get tough
there's humour and feistiness
to help lift the huff,

Most importantly though
undoubtedly so
is a four letter word
to help your life grow,

LOVE envelops all
captures and consumes
and by keeping me tucked up
somewhere safe in your rooms,

You'll have all you need
if you run out of steam
just open me up
and feel these things beam,

Let them fill the room
fill your heart, settle your mind

watch them join together
become intertwined,

Then close me up tight
and pop me away
so I can fill myself up, for use
another day.

Melanie Parry-Graham

THE BALLAD OF TWO

When we're doing what we're doing
When we're doing the do
The only thing I want to do, is do it with you
I'm licking your lips and it's tasting so sweet
You start kissing me all over from my head to my feet
You never looked so beautiful in the moonlit night
So I'm going to take my time and do it just right
Getting closer and closer, I can feel your heat
By the time it's all over, click rewind and repeat
As I take you to the place which is in your dreams
Better put a sign on the door
'Please Excuse the Screams'
Our eyes connect and our souls start synchronising
While our bodies entwine and begin harmonising
To the rhythm of love with a passionate beat
Wow! It's so hot, there's no need for the sheet
It's all for you, I'll do whatever you desire
Take you so high you'll see the fantasy transpire
Then go from reality to heaven on earth
I see by the smile, you're loving the rebirth

Peter Pearce

LOVE IS FALLING IN A POND

One day, in spring of Sixty-Eight
I suffered a most watery fate.
Who was that standing on the bank up there,
Mocking me with eyes that taunted and bewitched;
Hair so dark and flowing.
She said her name was Clare.

Smitten with a love so great I stood no chance,
The spell was cast, I was entranced, unknowing;
My world had been enriched.
We kissed a lot,
Then tied the knot.

Years they came and went.
Children four passed through our door
And by the spring of Ninety-Six
I was nigh on spent.

Now here we are in spring again,
Twelve years further down the road
To where the Reaper Grim awaits.
Her hair is not so black and straight
And mine has thinned to wispy grey.
Her eyes have dimmed a little.
But still light up the day.

So we'll fight him to the bitter end
With love and memories fond
Of spring in Nineteen-Sixty-Eight
When I fell in the pond.

Ben Corde

ETERNAL LOVE

There will never be another love like ours,
Faithful, true, without a doubt
Endless devotion, never a recrimination,
You could never ever be replaced
A love like yours could not flout...

Your eyes glow pools of faithfulness
Love wavers not a day
You know when I am feeling low
Showing me warmth of sunshine ray
A love like yours...

Every day is special as we share our life together
Always live in harmony
Whatever brings the weather
To be close is special
True love like ours...

You love to have a sweet caress
As I brush your shining hair,
You walk and swim and fly with me
Apart? We could not bear
With love like ours...

Your simple life is truly spent
A faithful friend, dependent love
Companionship, life hand in glove
Endless love, four-legged friend
Love of my life 'dog' should read 'god'
Endless love
A love like ours...

Meg Lewis

PRECIOUS MEMORIES

Chants of laughter can be heard afar
Children chanting and playing games
Innocence and beauty portrays
What a beautiful sight they are as I watch from my window
Like a nagging mother does
Holding hands, skipping and clapping
These are the memories of every mother's keepsake
As tears stream my face unknowingly I realise
How happiness can also be sadness to see them grow
To see them leave, to see their individuality
It's not all sad it's more proud
Forever a mother's heart will hold you
Forever she cradles you, no matter the age you will always be
The most precious gift she received
Parenting is never easy
Some days of smiles, some days of tears,
Days of laughter, days of naughty steps
Every step you grew me as a woman, every step you grew you
made my heart grow bigger
To my mother and father thank you for teaching me how to
become the woman I am today
To my children I love you.

Danielle Harris

ROMANTIC RENDEZVOUS

Marriage means more than a couple's caring contract
Establishing the way one another should act
It is from this day on you've to have and to hold
Shown by those nuptial bands of gold
Now that you have both decided to tie the knot
Please give this special synthesis all that you've got
No more bickering, you're together till the end
Even when you drive each other round the bend!
Consideration's the foundation for your wedlock
Unconditional love that's as solid as a rock
Heartfelt amity is shown on your uniting date
Such a fond-fusion with your no1 soulmate
With eternal loyalty that you both shall share
Passion is positively paramount for such a perfect pair
Matrimony keeps your spirits and dreams alive
Helps your desires and emotional state survive
Everlasting happiness you will always endeavour
Now you've found your friend for the future - forever.

TravsTales

4.37ISH

That's when I drift off with you,
waking again at 5.10.

With me cupping your z-shaped
body into mine we dozed away.
I'm sure we didn't dream because
when we woke you called the sleep perfect.

Just before getting in, after unclothing,
I'd put on Billie Holiday, taken the lip of the bed
for my seat, looked over and seen how your head
had parcelled itself in the cushions.

The low bedside lights softened the quilt about you.
A barking dog on the street out front
shifted and rippled you slightly.
When he quieted down you sighed and sang
a little along with Billie
for maybe half a bar or so.
Your scrunched mouth in half-sleep then set, like either
you were thinking of a question or showing
quiet surprise at the answer.
I took you in, beautiful, then nestled amid you,
and you wiggled around to better
let me be there too.

Fred M-G

INSIDE OF ME

There's no disgrace
In needing space
Space to live
Space to breathe
You can sit on a sofa
You can sit in a tree
You can be
Whoever you want to be
You can be warm
You can be open
You can be free
You can be inside of me
Deliberate redemption
Deliberate minds
You are so brutal
You are so kind
Can you sleep over
Can you be mine
In the passage of time
Visitation from a lover
From the past
It's a dilemma
It's a farce
You were so brittle
You were so hard
It was a tragedy
And so incongruous
Even before it did start
Swap your locks

For a shock
You've got cancer
And radiation is the block
We made love so to speak
And you died so suddenly
Just last week
And it was just time on a clock
That you couldn't stop
And sadly you passed on.

Geoffrey Medlicott

INFINITY

Once you're married, you think it's great
Playing at home in an up and coming estate
You've dieted, juiced and held your stomach in
You wore the dress and flashed your bling, but
Remember the moment, let me begin when your
Man was masculine and you laughed with him, his
Muscles bulged out, fun times begin, he was all
Body and you went to the gym, now you're too
Busy and not so slim, he's stressed out, his hair's
Gone thin. Where's the love that comes from within?
So he bought his missus a peace offering, a red
Mixing bowl and matching red bin, she chortled
With laughter and kissed him, he chased her
Upstairs, but the family hound wouldn't let 'em in
It may sound harsh and totally true, but the person
I married, was it the real you? The seasons are long, I'm
Fragile too. We don't need reasons to say I love you.

Angela Rachel Allen

I'M SORRY TOO

I'm sorry for not saying it first, when sometimes I really need to
And I know that sometimes it hurts but it doesn't mean that I
don't want to
And I may not say these words as often as I should
But that doesn't mean *I love you* any less than I do
I love you more from head to toe
And I know for sure that I should show it more
So, I'm saying *sorry* for all the times
When I've been wrong and you've been right
And I know you're going to like that line
Because you *do* tell me that all the time
*I love you*r honesty although sometimes it's hard to take
And *I'm sorry* for not always believing you right away
But at the end of the day *I love you* with all of my heart
Just like I have done from the very start.

Alston Buchanan

MY KIDS

I'm not a perfect parent,
But I try my best,
I keep my kids happy,
However my house is a mess,
I do things for them,
That teach them to be strong,
Even when I'm tired,
I do my best to carry on,
I help them out when they are stuck,
Give them kisses and hugs,
When they need that special touch,
For they are full of bugs,
I hide it when I'm in pain,
So they don't worry,
I get them to school,
There are times we have to hurry,
I wish sometimes they would stop growing,
For one day they won't always need me,
That day will be very hard,
When I have to let them be free,
So at the moment,
I'm going to hold them close,
Give them loads of memories,
That show I love them most,
So when that day does come,
They will always know,
I'm never that far away,
For them to come home.

Emily Sims

LOVE POEM

My love is like a perfect candle
Softly scented, with a comforting pose
Lighting up the all-pervading darkness
Lifting my spirits, holding me close

The candle burns, my heart affirms that she's the one
The candle burns, my eyes concur, I am undone

It is not electric, there is no switch
This light is constant, warm and rich
Guiding, leading, hold my hand
The beauty in the sounds of a loving band

The candle burns, I feel her holding me in her heart
The candle burns, entwined forever from the start

I feel your warmth, steady, and holding
The glow shines out, intensely enfolding
Ever present, today, tomorrow and before
Never changing, always, always my amour

The candle burns, I wonder at this feeling in my soul
The candle burns, she is the one that makes me whole.

Richard Roberts

PRECIOUS MOMENTS

Memories etched on a canvas and stretched
Pictures recorded in time
We shouldn't have dared but we did and we shared
Secrets so few but sublime

Memories past that never could last
Each an unsurpassed moment to me
Days long gone by and the meeting of eyes
And hearts that longed to be free

Memories of gold in a world bleak and cold
Diamonds on a shoreline of sand
The joy of pure magic the moments of madness
Could never be held in the hand

Memories fade to step out of the shade
Like islands in an ocean of blue
Where deep waters swirl and tides rip and curl
And where wreckage can tear you in two.

Memories etched on a canvas and stretched
Pictures recorded in time
We shouldn't have dared but we did and we shared
Precious moments stilled for all time

Keith Nuhrenburg-Wilson

MY ROCK

I sit and watch him for a while
The way he looks, the way he smiles
His brown eyes always expressive
Those soft gentle lips so impressive
So caring, helpful, going that extra mile
My goodness we always laugh so loud
He really is special, stands out in a crowd
We got through the bad times
We are going through the great times
He shows kindness in so many ways
Never changing, ever helpful all the days
Always worried when I'm unwell or ill
Checking to see if I'm warm enough if there is a chill
He is an animal lover, caretaker, homemaker
Loves to grow fresh, makes a pie, what a baker
We have been together a long while
I know what makes him tick what makes him smile
I've always loved him, his quirky ways, his style
Now still in love and retired everything is so worthwhile.

Kelly Stevens

ENDURING VALENTINE

What to thee do I compare?
I would not dare
Or see why
To take pen to paper.
For considering you and I
What actually is there
For us to keep
On turning pillows
But forever lasting sleep?

Yet running deeper
Than younger hearts feel
When starting out on fitful flights
Is our synchronous beat
Even on quiet nights,
And now our bodies
Grow old and tired,
Though we have no children sired
Or legacy to leave mankind,
We,
We are together fulfilled,
And of corresponding mind.

As nature's forces measure
In strengths of great and weak,
So I turn to nature's gift;
Our force, our bond.
Could one possibly seek
Any other just as strong?

I imagine only emptiness
If nature takes you
And you are gone.

George McDermid

PURPOSE ATTAINED

Discovery of love springs ineffable vivacity.
As love grows, time goes not fast nor slow.
Not a moment will there be in time fore or aft,
Not a time will there be; the universe could deny our love.
Infinite love: around my neck, in my heart; love's tenacity.
Life forever changed; to you, one worth living, I do owe.
Over my life, my happiest moments; when I was the reason you
laughed.
Virtuous in nature, from dirt flourishes the lily rising above.
Everlasting is our bond, it is and so always will be.
Salubrious influence, my path has a rapturous glow.
Stormy seas makes great sailors, though we shall be each other's
life raft.
United by circumstance, life's raison d'être we claim a part of.
Eternal adoration is your right, bestowing so, my heart's delight.

Danni Schilling Day

LIFE IS LIKE AN OLD OAK TREE

Life is like an old oak tree,
It blossoms and grows and then becomes complete.

Many people pass through our lives
And make us more knowledgeable, brighter and wise.

If we learn from our mistakes,
We can carry on and then make our big break.

Happiness is my epidemic, I believe
If you give a lot you will soon start to receive.

The less we worry about silly little things,
We will soon achieve and start to win.

Most of us do not recognise our potential,
If we stay positive, we may even become influential.

It stands to reason that the happier we become,
Life will start falling into place and become much more fun.

Never underestimate the potential within,
This is the first place for one to begin.

Helen Pigeon

A FRIEND, A SOUL, A LOVER

When your tears fall softer than the rain
And it seems memories are all that remain
When the night has given way to the day
And you forget the words you wanted to say
Don't let yesterday become tomorrow
As you search for happiness in sorrow.

When love seem as though it is all but gone
And you feel as though you can't carry on
Look for the heart that has always been there
And you will always have someone to care
We all need a heart to hold
Someone to protect us when it's cold.

All I can say, as my words come to an end
In these loving words to you I send
Search for a friend to love, a soul to treasure
Through all the pain; through all the pleasure
To laugh and cry with one another
We all need that friend, that soul, that lover.

Graham Connor

MY LOVE

I don't have to say 'I love you'
You see it in my eyes
Mellow and mellifluous
Gentle as midnight moon
Glowing with my love for you.

You feel it in my lips
Soft like rose petals in bloom
Tender yet hot in touch with yours
Hotter than the midday sun

You find it in my embrace for you
Passionate like a passion fruit
Succulent, you feel it flow
Like a stream of milk and honey

It's in my hugs for you
When you are down and out
And the world against you
You find them ever comforting

That is my love for you, my love.

Tell me now, do I need to say 'I love you'?
When the angels in the firmament
Whisper my love for you
Boundless, endless, till the end of time.

A Jamil

WATER

I had another revelation while watching her
swim: something of the properties of water.
You see, as long as it isn't kept in a closed
containment, water shifts and embraces you,
compromises for the existence of your space,
evolving in harmony, a synonymous description
of the forces between gravity, the earth and
her body, all at once.

The way it playfully diffracts light into the contortions
of space and lays out the fundamentals of colour
into perfect order, from the cool depths of violet to
the feverish heat of the red, without any sense of
confusion

and how when in it, she seems so much closer to
weightlessness, unrestrained as she explores

Yes, now I understand: love, is metaphysical water.

Pj Armstrong

MEMORIES AND WISDOM

When a family loses a member,
Love shared by, and with, a different agenda,
Comfort comes in so many different ways,
Knowing the depth of feeling one conveys.

Time has a mysterious type of kindness,
Contributes a warmth of understanding which is timeless,
Emotions recognised with depths of feeling,
Are exchanged with instant loving reasoning.

Recalling moments in life past, but not gone,
Restores a treasured memory stimulates warmth to belong,
To belong to a past that brought a unity of love,
Emulates a wisdom which transmits from above.

As time generates into a number of years,
The memory of yesterday amid times of tears,
One accepts the privilege of a memory's gift,
To share and value the time given, emotions will uplift.

Lorna Tippett

NIGHT SKY - LOST LOVE?

Why is the night sky always so dark?
When the moon gave its silvery glow,
you said, 'It's time to leave now';
but I didn't want you to go.
You told me you no longer needed me,
that you didn't really care.
I closed my eyes as I listened;
when I opened them you were not there.
Tomorrow the sun will rise again,
to shine in a sky so blue;
but for now I'll sit in the shadows
and wait right here for you.
I'll think of the past, those happy times
when we laughed together, you and I.
Then I'll face this time of sadness;
I'll cover my face when I cry.
Tonight, I'll dream you still love me,
for you lied when you said, 'I don't care.'
I know when I wake in the morning,
you, my love, will be there.

Mary Chapman

MUSE

You can't leave, you can't go,
There's so many things about you that I am yet to know,
I can't say goodbye and I know I can't forget,
I'm just not finished writing about you yet.

Please stay, I need you so,
I love you and I'm feeling things I've never felt before,
I don't want to move on, I'll only have regret,
I don't want to stop writing about you yet.

Each day, you can be sure,
I wake up missing you more than the day before,
It breaks my heart and you can bet,
I've so much more to write about you yet.

It's true, my heart is sore,
It's found it broken often but to you I can't say no,
I can't give up, my mind is set,
I won't give up writing about you yet.

Stephanie Simpson

LOVE ETERNAL

Love eternal means so many things,
This love for you makes my whole world sing.
Lifted up as if I were on wings
Love eternal you are everything.
There are so many loves in my life,
Love for my brothers cuts like a knife.
Love of friends, with this throw of a dice.
Love for you, you're the love of my life.
A daughter's love is hard to compare,
A different love makes the angels stare.
I carry it with me everywhere.
I carry you too, you're always there.
Love eternal means the world to me,
You're in my heart I wish you could see
How I love you, never set me free.
I love you darling, eternally.
Is it an obsession, you tell me
I close my eyes and it's you I see
Yes, here in my heart eternally
Obsessed, with you perpetually.

Janet Boxall

BECAUSE

You were my strength when I was weak
You give me back what they took from me
You were my air so I could breathe
You give me love that was hard to beat

You stood by me in the dark crowds... and
You picked me up when I was down
You give me hope and let me win... and
You showed me the joys that love can bring

You were the sight into my eyes
You dried my tears and told me not to cry
You give me back what they took from me
You stood by me and now I'm feeling free

You put the words back into my mouth
Although some tried to take me down south
Now I know you're the love I've found
Because you turned my world around

Now I know you're the one for me
And this is because you love me.

Yvette Avonda Layne

A LOVE SONG SONNET

They really don't write love songs any more
Not like they did just after the last war
The fifties crooners sang out from the soul
The sixties gave more than just rock and roll

'The Look of Love' and 'I'm a Believer'
'Unchained Melody', would never leave her
The Kinks they sang, 'You Really Got Me Babe'
While Dylan's 'Lay Lady Lay'... got us laid.

'When a Man Loves a Woman' don't ask why
'My Girl' ran the 'River Deep, Mountain High'
She just 'Can't Help Falling in Love with You'
But 'Memories' make us feel 'Misty Blue'

So, until they write like they did from way
back when. 'I'll Never Fall in Love Again'.

Lee Montgomery-Hughes

SMILE

She gently arrives with her naturally gracious flow,
Like a sunbeam breaking through the clouds she warms us with
her glow.

She delivers her beauty so innocently with a subtle flick of the hair,
Twinkling like a sky of stars in a moment you're lost in her glare.

Eyes that glow with truth and passion with each blink she draws
you inside,
Like staring into a kaleidoscope you get lost in the beauty she
hides.

She moves around like a flower in the wind and her petals glisten
in the light,
Her stunning form sways in the breeze as she dances into the
night.

She moves into each moment with so much class and grace
And when she's gone she leaves the perfect memory...

The smile from our last embrace.

Stuart Wells

WAITING AT NIGHT

what do I know about her?
she is someone I did not know
I want to wait
for the sake of waiting
you pour everything
into the cup of the imagination
forty-three years now
these empty night hours
empty of all a human being
has to offer
I did not know her
I wait for the time
that has run out
for the women I remember
who crossed my path
with their feline grace
honing in on me
with malevolent intent
wanting to make off with what
I had to offer
you I love boundlessly
I know you uninterruptedly
I see into your souls
my hand caresses you
it is time for me to leave
I did not know her
I did not know you

which is why I waited
why I thought of you
to no avail as ever

Simon Warren

A GIFT FROM ABOVE TO SHOW YOU ARE LOVED

A rose bush in the garden
You planted in memory of me
Full of buds and you wake up to
Find the roses dancing in the
Bright morning sunshine
I send you this
A gift from above
To show you are loved

A river with the trees hanging over it
And as the leaves fall and float
Out to sea you can see
My spirit dancing from rock to rock
I send you this
A gift from above
To show you are loved

The robin sitting on a branch
Looking in your window
On a cold December morning
To see you are OK
I send you this
A gift from above
To show you are loved

Dedicated to everyone
Who has an angel

To send them
A gift from above
To show you are loved.

Alison M Bass-Hunt

BREATH OF LIFE

Is it love that runs deep through my veins,
pumping blood to my metaphoric heart?
Each beat resuscitates, regenerates and revitalises
the darkest crevices of my soul.
It is a medicine, sweet and tender;
absorbed by true love's kiss
and travels through my bloodstream lightning fast,
as though my body craves it.
The warmth it brings spreads right through
the tips of my fingers and toes;
and as she holds her hands in mine,
I know I warm her too.
A pulsing glow emits around her
awakening my synapses.
As she kisses me again
a ball of air rises towards my chest,
she has breathed life into me!
I think this is what love feels like.
I'll never know who I was before her.
Please don't break my heart again.

Jade Kelly

REMINDINGS

Starlight and sunshine beams,
Dazzled diamonds golden dreams,
Flower clouds with big silver linings,
Aoife's eyes and all of her shinings,
The warmth of a fire in wondrous surroundings,
This lovely poem and its really crumby rhymings!
The sparkly sea the awe of her beauty,
Ice cream and chocolate but nothing too fruity!
Autumn's rusty reds spring's beautiful bloom,
Winter's glittery frost to summer's full moons,
The mind-bending stars and all of their glory,
The wonder of the earth and its billion year story,
Slippers of rubies the technicolour scene,
One click and you're home with me and our dreams,
Just a few of the things that belong to you,
That remind me of you that are part of you.

Anthony Robert Aked

BOOK LOVER'S DATE NIGHT

Looking for love at the library?
Browse the Mills & Boons and find
Me ready, waiting, anticipating
Your caress upon my spine.

Take me down from off the shelf
Turn my pages, come on in.
Just you and me – there's no one else.
Let the tale of love begin.

Borrow me, take me home.
Glass of wine, forget your troubles,
Candles lit, relax, unwind,
Read me in your bath of bubbles.

Let your imagination free.
All the worries of today
In fantasies of passion gone
In foam and fiction, washed away.

And so to bed, all snuggled up,
Read me through, from cover to cover.
Then, take me back: I'm loaned, not owned,
And now am promised to another.

Robert Barker

THE WEDDING

I've heard it said that marriage is somehow out of date,
And promises are quite enough between man and his mate,
That solemn vows in legal terms should be things of the past,
For we believe when we are you, our love is sure to last.

But still we want the world to know we hold each other dear,
And take congratulations from our friends all gathered here.

For Tanya and for Roger, this day will always be
A day to treasure all life through, a happy memory.
And pledges made will never fade between two so united.
Whose flame of love burns always bright, as when it first ignited.

And so whatever fate may bring, their love will still remain.
Together they will see it through, and share the joy or pain.

Frank Flower

UNCONDITIONAL SENSUALITY

Sensuality is not exclusive to the young
Physicality of youth does not last for long
Attracted by her stunning countenance
In the early years, lust fuelled our romance

Longevity brings its own strengths to the game
Footsteps of my woman always sound the same
I know her stride, I can tell when she is near
That's the way it is; after over forty years

To see her smile is a sight to treasure
Her happiness brings me unbridled pleasure
From domination, both of us exempt
Familiarity does not breed contempt

As time goes by, appearance less important
Ardour eases, but never will lie dormant
Listening to her heartbeat over decades
Unconditional love, needs no more to be said.

David Eager

DEARLY DEPARTED MUM

(In memory of Kathleen Patricia (Penny) Maddrell, 1931-2008)

My dearly departed Mum.
Forever you will
speak to my heart each day.
I miss you beside.
That touch of hands, eyes and lips.
Whose words live through me:

It's vital to give yourself
the freedom to live.
In peace, I'd create for you
chances of dreams, hopes.
My gifts of love I leave you.
It's now up to you.

My dearly departed Mum.
Forever you will speak to my heart.
Each day I miss you beside,
that touch of hands.
Eyes and lips whose words
live through me:

It's vital.
To give yourself the freedom
to live in peace.
I'd create for you chances of dreams.
Hopes, my gifts of love, I leave you.
It's now up to you.

Simon Maddrell

AFRICAN LOVE

What is love?
Who is love?
I am a poet
But when it comes to love
Words seem to go astray
For love comes in many forms.
Romantic love very rarely stays
So I banish it, from my life.
But I am so very much in love
With the African smiles
Oh how I love those smiles
Oh how I love those children
Their smiles magnify my soul
I have penned so many poems
For their smiles bring me joy
Daddy Ray they used to call him
As they climbed on him and hugged him so
Now it is Prince Harry
They love him, and he loves them too
Lady Diana gave them a lifetime of love
My love for these children
Is more than words can say
For their magical smiles
Enhanced me on a cold winter's day.

Carolie Cole Pemberton

THE DREAM IN ME

Love is a powerful gift
One that can swell up inside your body
And your heart is thumping with joy
Until you say goodbye
That is when your heart breaks

As you share your first kiss
Under the romance of the starlit sky
This is the dream that I dream
Will it ever come true?

As I wade through the water
And come to the shore
I see an unknown figure
Is the dream to become reality?

I will never find out
For my eyes flutter open
And my heart is still beating
But my spirit is still high

For there are red roses by my bed
And a letter is sealed with hope
Is this dream to become reality?
I will find out one day.

Lucie Prosser

CLOUDED LOVE

The weight of the world is not one that heaven can endure,
Instead I feasted my eyes upon a raven,
I watched him as he pondered, agitated, and severed by his claw.
He flew so hard with love so tame,
Yet inside a man hidden, craving, living in vain.
She cut across him with her clouds so soft, the heart of the dead,
but the mind of the lost.
She aimlessly floated as he flew purposely in her way,
Love has no boundaries, crossing paths, come what may.
She precipitated a human form so empowered,
He transformed from a bird, to a man, no longer a coward.
Become as one as Zeus once claimed,
A human with four arms and four legs, disconnected in half,
Forever looking for one in the same.

Priya Yoganathan

WANTING MORE

I always wanted to be loved; today, I'm not so sure!
Had silly notions when young but not now, I am mature.
My love causes me anguish. How much pain can I endure?
Often I put in lots of my time and then so much more.

But available men in my life will never commit,
They will not compromise, no, not even a tiny bit.
sometimes I feel so let down I'm depressed and I am unfit,
As my search for love continues, I lose the meaning of it.

Only someone in this position, could know what I feel,
Want relationships to last forever, to be real!
To make date arrangements without needing a royal seal,
But I won't beg for affection or to men my dreams reveal.

Sue Mullinger

WITH LOVE TO MY CHILDREN

Baby pink and powder blue
Always remember that I love you... Two

My life began when I had you.
I gave you life, you gave me mine,
Always there right on time.

Baby pink and powder blue
Always remember that I love you... Two

You're the ones who helped me through
'What goes on behind closed doors!'
The pain and illness too.

Baby pink and powder blue
Always remember that I love you... Two

Together through thick and thin.
You are my lifeline, my hope
My kith and kin...

We have a special bond, binding us together without restricting us
To infinity and beyond...

Hilary Ankers

OUTSIDE

you are a slow-moving pendulum
caught-up in my hindsight
a web tangled misconception
wrapped around the stem cells
of every illusion I never want to let go of
a dream weaver, fighting my nightmares

the seconds falling into dust
an air spirit between my ribs
all of the wishes I forgot to make
because everything else got in the way
the flesh on my bones, my blood...

skin that tortures so eloquently
fragile fixation, fading in and out
sometimes, I am just a ghost
and you are the tangible part of me

my corporeal weight. I am immortal
without those broken parts
the stars in my veins are still with you

Anita Wakeham

NEW YEAR

(For my husband, Dave Underhill, who passed 22/04/2016)

The love of my life has passed away,
This has broken my heart in two.

The vow 'Until death us do part'
Is always in the future, not now

It may be a new year now,
But it does not lessen my grief.

I will forever be stuck in 2016,
And will never again be complete.

I will never 'move on' as they say,
For no one can ever replace him.

We've been there, done that, so I will be,
Content to live with my memories.

It will never stop me from crying,
And feeling so very alone.

But I will never even think of moving,
For he is everywhere in our home.

Susan Olivia Leyton Underhill

I LOVE YOU

Love is certainly in the air,
precious time we share.
Doing jobs together with care,
thinking of one another's welfare.

We have two loving lads,
who enjoy drawing and writing in notepads.
Playing football, wearing shin pads,
and like to have a kick around with Mum and Dad.

We have fun in the snow, with a snowball fight,
and plan our holidays with delight.
We enjoy days in the sunlight,
and spend time outside on a summer's night.

Every day with you is an absolute pleasure,
and you, I will always treasure.
We are ready for a day's adventure,
and excited about what lies ahead in our future...

Adrian Bullard

LOVE

All kinds of love
Fantasy and reality
All kinds of love
Kings and queens
Bow at their knees
To greet love at its honour.
All kinds of love
Family and friends
All kinds of love
Light meaning day
And dark meaning night
All kinds of love the stars twinkle at night
All kinds of love
Real and fake
All kinds of love
Hurt and pain
From the everlasting rain
That hits down on the harsh ground.
All kinds of love
Loving you was the best I could do
All kinds of love
Means more than just three words
All kinds of love
More than just a cliché of music.
All kinds of love
All kinds of light.

Leanne Drain

EVER THINE

My most precious, precious love -
I hear you calling me.
Through a chillingly cold night -
I hear you beloved.

I want to reach out to you -
Cool your fevered brow -
Quench your thirst
And feed your nightly hunger.

Fight on - beloved.
I will hear your voice -
Even a million miles away.
I am yours - until the end of time.

Two lost souls -
Thrown to the waves on a tempestuous
Sea of life.
Yet love conquers
All suffering -
Heals all ills.

Fight on beloved -
I hear you calling me.
As time stands still -

For all those

Who love.

Nina Graham

LOVE OF MY HEART

After the last pale moon has risen
And the stars close their eyes for one last time,
After the night-winds cease to cry
And I have spilt my ink upon this rhyme.
After the aspen trees hush their singing,
And the world shivers as the doors close,
The roar of the ocean stills and is silent,
The petals wither in the heart of the rose.
After the sky floats down to Earth,
Earth ephemeral sighs in the night
The soft pulse of her heart grows faint,
As I commence to enter into the light.
Slow breeze from the bay, wild memories,
Enter and take stock before I depart.
My last ever thought will be of you,
My one, my only, Love of my heart.

Lorraine DeSousa

LEAVES

The trees
Bereft of love
Leaves through
Door of storm
On the same breeze
Whence carried
The idea of them
From the first pollen kiss
Honeyed sap lip
Of spring's sweet breath.
Arthritic knuckled branches
In painful stretch
Bend to embrace
Their memory
In the rapture of your absence.
Cold batters bare faced,
Bark. Pockmark lined
By years of unsuspecting love.
Falls
For same promises
Till time is up
and never
Do the leaves of your love
Stay with me.
Old tree, no fool like me.
Gleeful wonder at the sunlight of your
Return. Whispers
Never leave me again.
Old tree.

Jonathan Lais

TWO YEARS

The last two years I have been short of love,
Wounded – literally – alone, bereft,
Yearning to be offered something soft,
And mourning everything I did not have.
When this passed, I was hardened, steeled and cold,
Flayed skin turned marble; I was statuesque,
Strong and hostile, I would never ask
Again for something soft to loves untold.
But lately I would like to have been held,
To feel at ease with someone who is *fun* –
To choose a little better, to be bold,
To banish thoughts of one who's not my one.
And if I find someone, well maybe then –
In two years' time, I'll be in love again.

Caitlin Coulson

A HEART'S VIEW

A vision, a sight, a view from the heart,
Are we meant to be together or forever be apart?
A feeling of passion, imagination and dreams
Forever tormented, misread and teased

To strike on a heart so gentle and kind
To play with emotions and confuse the mind.
The hardest of people have feelings as well
Though they don't wear it for all to see and tell

Scared of what's coming, what's gone, what might have been
Scared of the future without true feelings being shared and seen
Dig deep in your heart and soul and say what you felt
The person you're scared of losing may be feeling the same as you
as well!

Samantha Shelford

ST VALENTINE'S DAY

Shows the spirit of martyrdom
In the annual scourging of partners,
And lovers, with the failed expectations
Imposed by mass market media.
How generic and trite every 'hearted' card
And proclamation of love, as if words,
Any more than flowers, could
Ever say it right, could ever
Tell it like it is. Even the Romantics,
For all their poetry and freed up
Eighteenth-century passions, somehow
Seem to overdose on exaggerations
Of love. But as for me, I look at you,
And feel a gentle, soppy grin settle
Inside my head, and also on my face,
Conscious that I am allowed to be
This happy, just to be where you are.

Christopher Sleeman

A LOVE STORY

Mosaic perceptions
Same chain of events. The day is kaleidoscopic
Bonfire, rainbow coloured robes!
A wedding celebration. Dancing
Hennaed hands;
A serpent, they make
In the sky.

Hearts are meant to be of the same fabric.
Hers is a glass candy, his is archaic.
Yet... yet... yet...
They make it work somehow
Still together years to come.

Cellulite of his heart is the colour of rust.
In the eye of her mind.
She is an artist:
Rust is transformative.
Cellulite of her heart is kaleidoscopic.
He is a visionary.
The colour is transformative.
And that is love. Love. Love.

Yasemin Balandi

IN THE POOL WITH OUR POOCHES

(A poem to eternal love)

I love to swim with my doggy.
It really is so nice!
Folks ask about their pee and poo,
And fleas; their ticks, their lice,
And of vials and lyme disease,
And leptospirosis,
Serovar canicola
And toxocara canis
But they're worth the risking.
We all must die you know!
And bathing with our pooches,
Is a grand way to go!
And when en masse, our dogs dive in,
It's splashy, hairy, muddy,
And we get scratched and bitten
And the pool turns all bloody!
But the highlight's swimming synchro,
With our gorgeous canine chums,
Making really pretty circles
With our noses up their bums!

Edward Lyon

ETERNAL LOVE

Love is just another word but oh so different from the rest
Just its sound is like a soft caress
It is a word we can use so flippantly
I love that car, I love that dress, I'm sure that you can guess the rest.
Eternal love is such a special thing it's not a diamond or a ring.
For true love is like eternal spring.
Our family and our friends, all those we love, we hold them in a strong yet gentle glove.
But the price of true love is very high
For if one you love slips from that glove
The pain you feel so deep inside I cannot begin to describe.
Yet I would rather bear that pain than to say that I could never love again.

PoGem

FIRST LOVE

I had read the novel
Then I saw you in the ballroom -
My Lorna Doone.

So young, slender and graceful
Your face radiated innocence.

Slowly, you walked toward me
As if I had a remote control
And you were responding.

I remember that coral dress
Caressing your curves
Complementing the flush on your cheeks.

You drew close - noticed me.

Who can explain the mystery?
That moment of enchantment and exquisite delight
The captivating magnetism -
The meeting of eyes.

You smiled and snatched my heart
The sun broke through the clouds.

Jonathan Bryant

LOVE DOESN'T NEED A RESUME

Love doesn't need a resume.

It's not a corporate deal.
It's not a business agreement.
It's not numbers at a till.
It's not colouring inside the lines
with crayons black and white.
It's not ticking, selecting or filling
Boxes -

Love doesn't always rhyme.

It's not magnolia muted walls
on a mortgaged property
It's not medicine prescribed -
When we feel unhappy.
It's not riding up an escalator
and casually stepping off.
It's not a product advertised -

Love doesn't live in a shop.

Jean Cable

ETERNAL LOVE

How I've loved, how I've lost,
How I've loved, how I've thrown it away,
How I've loved, how I've been physically hurt,
How I've loved, how I've been mentally hurt.
Built a wall, as big as the one in China,
Around my own self
Independent woman
Didn't need no great love
I survived
Along came my grandaughters
And I'm in love all over again
Pure unconditional love
They melt my heart
How I've loved, how I've won,
How I've loved, how I've held on,
How I've loved and physically healed,
How I've loved and mentally healed.

Sammi

MY HEARTFELT REVELATION

She is like a home and a vacation,
With each word she speaks, every action she takes,
She has me in a feeling of deep sensation,
She can see by now she is my inspiration,
Using her artistic hands to mould my imagination,
Our own type of love being our beautiful creation.

How hard to believe that when she met me
I was in a state of fragmentation,
Yet somehow she fixed me needing no preparation,
There was no hesitation for it, nor explanation,
All it took was for her to hold my hand to feel my longed
fascination,
Being to me, my arrived longing of speculation,
She is my heartfelt revelation.

Daniel Link

WITH LOVE TO YOU I WRITE THIS

With love to you I write this
And from my heart these words I say
Your love and understanding
Are what makes each brand new day

Your hand on mine, your gentle smile
From lips so soft and warm
Your eyes reflecting all that's good
All bring the sun each morn

My darling life for me would end
Should you decide to leave
Without you standing at my side
Each day and night I'd grieve

So take and take and hold this love I give
Yes, hold it captive in your heart
And we'll walk life's road together
And know peace, at each day's start.

Don Woods

YOU DRIVE ME INSANE

You make my worst days worse,
You make my best days better.
I hate you passionately, disgustingly,
I love you hopelessly, endlessly.

I wish I didn't love you to the point of sickness,
Why can't I be normal?
And care less, like you?

Our love is a parasite.
It plagues my entire mind and body.
They say love and hate are the same,
I became unbalanced with the smallest gust of wind,
Tipping me between extremities.

If I loved you less I may be well,
I definitely would not be around,
But I am afraid that I do love you,
So much, I am now insane.

Imogen Swash

DIVORCE

Although you have not died
You have left and gone
I cannot reach the part of you
I loved for so, so long
I see you and you look the same
But inside you're not there
I look and look and miss you so
And sometimes shed a tear
And even though I am OK
And even though I live
And even though my heart is warm
And I choose to forgive
Even after all of this
I sometimes feel so low
I look but cannot find you there
No matter where I go
And even though it's all OK
We have both moved on
I miss the man I used to love
He went, he's lost, he's gone.

Rebekah Hoare-Bond

HOW DO I LOVE YOU?

(With apologies to Elizabeth Barrett Browning)

How do I love you? Well now let me see...
I love you despite the depth of passion
you hold for football, cricket and Top Gear
(though Jeremy Clarkson does my head in).
I love you even when you have man flu
and drive me to distraction with your moans.
I love you though you always must be right.
I love you though you're usually quite wrong.
I love you with a passion never felt
before, nor could I ever find again.
I love you as both best friend and lover,
my second half, my significant other,
my husband one day should you choose to ask.
I shall love you even better with a ring.

Tracy Davidson

MY SON, MY BOY, MY JOY

I love you more than words can say
My love gathers each and every day
Like the tides pull in the oceans
The waves lap at the shore
My love gathers more and more

All the stars in the sky
All the questions people ask, oh why?
This doesn't sum up my love for you
Oh son, it's true
You're the world to me
My deepest passion
My strongest thoughts
My rawest emotions

I'm blessed to have you in my life
You're my miracle, my dream come true
I just wouldn't want to live my life without you
I love you always my boy, love Mamma.

Susan Kaye

ETERNAL LOVE

In the world of Art, love is presented:
In the shape of a scented flower,
Or perhaps the sound of a beautiful babbling brook,
The feel of the sun shining on the lawn,
The sweetness of birds whistling through the summer trees,
Or the grandeur of classical music.
Love is pretty with pleasant sounds and wonderful scents.
How easy must eternal love be?

Love is dirty nappies with a dreadful smell,
Skint knees accompanied by melodramatic wailing,
Stroppy teenagers indignantly complaining and
Marital bickering. Absolute acceptance.
Eternal love may not be sweet but it is strong.

Mary Anne Moore

GRACE II

Deep beneath the darkening waves of the sea
Where no silence may be found
The torrents and flow of watery currents
Embed upon a chest of steel.
Madness grows like smelted glass
Fragile to be fractured, or
Blown into some inconsequential shape
By nameless, faceless sands.
It calls to the oceans like
A beating heart in a glass chest:
I love you, I love you, I love you,
Are all I've ever needed to know.
And waves grow silent and still;
Like a moment between morning and dawn
When seas and skies are timeless and blue,
And I'll love you always, forever.

Mustafa Al-Maree

COLD

We spend all week
passing each other like shadows.
Polite, seven years on.
Is this what they mean?
Not some dramatic bust up
but a quiet descent into
'No, no, after you',
'If you don't mind',
'I'm very well, thank you'.

Night. After a day outside time
where we've remembered what was
and is no longer.
In the cold, I share your duvet,
take my place beneath
what was once half mine.
In the dark you mumble I love yous
which only come to fruition
outside consciousness.
By morning the duvet's gone.

Katharine Goda

KEYS TO MY HEART

You hold the keys to my heart
To which now I've come to realise
You did from the very start
Solo journeys travelled
And lessons in life have been learnt
But to each other we have finally returned
Older and wiser
Our lives more simplified
Looking to rekindle a love
That through these many years has survived
A once beautiful romance
Surely deserves one more chance
Though time has elapsed
We were never meant to be apart
Through all the years of absence
I've finally realised...
It's only you
That ever held the keys to my heart.

Paula Holdstock

VALENTINE SONNET NO 1

I often wonder if you are of this earth,
The title of Angel would better fit
As beauty was yours since you claimed it at birth
And never since has a brighter light been lit.
True love personified as I live and breathe,
A transcendent being in you I've found
And so our union makes others believe
That such love is neither chained nor bound.
Our love hath inspired, a flame hath been passed
But no spark was needed to start our love fire,
We were born for each other and built to last,
Our love flows like brooks and blooms like the briar.
Now we lie in each other's loving embrace
And know that no sorrow shall we ever face.

Kierran Garner

WHEN?

When shall we meet again
To share a stolen hour?
When shall we meet again
In our own secret bower?
When shall we meet again
To shower kiss after kiss?
When shall we meet again
For our sweet moments of bliss?
When shall we meet again
To embrace with caresses and sighs?
When shall we meet again
To claim love's richest prize?

The sea may stand in our way,
The sea may flow without end,
Time may be our enemy,
Time may be our friend.

Time and tide may keep us far apart,
But we both live on in the other's heart.

Denis Bruce

PAST LIVES

Sometimes I want to believe
That in past lives
You and I
Were sisters, lovers
Parent, friend

That the joy
Of knowing you
Be not confined
To the narrow span
Of just one life

So when this life is done
We meet in the Bardo
And join in laughter
At our follies
And shared fun

But perhaps this life
Is all we have?
So I will treasure
Every precious memory
Each moment we share

And hold tight
To cords of friendship
And sweet
Chords of love
As unique as you and I.

David Babatunde Wilson

NATURAL DEVOTION

A seed, a little leaf,
A stem of quiet surprise -
Not disbelief
But, as the dew dries,
A morning's sweet relief

A blossoming of trust,
A slow sunrise,
A glimmer of the dust
Of butterflies

A dawning sense of nearness,
New and kind,
A gentle glow of dearness
Intertwined

A morning's wordless knowing,
Warm and bright,
A certainty of glowing -
Full sunlight.

Then, unrehearsed, 'I love you',
'Yes, I know',
Shining like the dew
At this cockcrow.

Philippa Elmhirst

ETERNAL LOVE

To love and be loved in return
There's nothing to compare
When the one I trust my heart with
Shows me just how much they care
The fire burns brighter in my soul
Whenever they are near
In the knowledge that they're by my side
Through happiness and tears

No matter what life's journey
Or the trials along the way
While my heart beats for another
I'll stay safe and out harm's way
And as the years pass slowly by
Our bodies may decline
But my heart beats just as strong for you
As yours will do for mine

Nina Thilo

MIS-

When the skin is torn
A craggy scab rises
To protect from the outside
What is raw within.

When foundations are shaken
Our 'self' loathed and forsaken
The face we portray
All we do and all we say
To keep that wound hidden away.

When the heart breaks
Gnarling scars
Pain so deep
Felt through every beat.
The muscle contracts
Tearing the wound
Beating strong
Pulling anew
Every
single
beat.
Invisible to all.

Time cannot touch
The heart's grief call.

K Mork

AN INVITATION

Eternal love invites
- insists a presence;
more than just a glimpse.

An entrance made in
prairies of the mind;
to lift a heart.

Another's eyes
expressing care;
a voice beloved.

Words or music
that caress, retained;
and new memory.

Nature's voice;
that harmonises;
but has ruthless strength.

Eternal rhythm;
- sunrise, morning;
evening, night.

To caress,
that inner being;
which feels, sees;
eternal love.

Sam Grant

LOVINGLY IN RETROSPECT

Lovingly I let him go
And wander on my many levels,
We opened boxed up wounds and weapons
When dawn broke, in my heart he sat and settled.

Nestled in our crippled spaces,
Craving affection through abject discord.

When we walked and reached the end of my hands
Gripped lovingly, so lovingly and struggling,
With tension choking open lesions
And trauma piercing crated mistakes until,
There was nothing left but shreds of distrust.

But lovingly, I let him go
And wandered back out to the earth.

Sian Cheung

ETERNAL LOVE

Often the nostrum is just a touch, the inkling of having someone
by your side,
Then why does my heart dither when I fancy for a future stride.

When does somatic disunion define the fate of a feeling; so pure,
Even when every step I take; every move I make is to make her
lure.

Why can't words be replete to describe what's at heart,
Because I know deep down that neither of us is ready to be apart.

So why do these disparate emotions take a toll on me?
For my love was always meant to be eternal and free!

Sonakshi Mittal

MY HEART AND SOUL UNDONE

You took the petals of my rose,
Removed each of my layers,
Exposed my inner private thoughts,
Revealed my inner players.

Extracted purest honesty,
Stripped my soul of any lies,
My open book now free to read,
You undid all my ties.

Broke down all of my defences,
Reached inside my inner core,
Touched my spirit and my senses,
Internally you saw it all.

Secret thoughts no longer held,
My heart and soul undone,
All of my pain was then expelled,
And now my fears are gone.

Christine Carol Burrows

MUMMY'S BIRTHDAY RAINBOW

My mummy sent a gift to me
I could not feel but I could see,
For here, upon my outstretched hand,
At once appeared a rainbow's band.

Our mummy's birthday is today,
We went to lay a sweet bouquet,
Our mummy passed three years ago
But she still loves us, this we know.

Sometimes, on important days,
We have been blessed by coloured rays,
She lets us know that she is near
By sending us a sign so clear.

Far better than a pot of gold
Are precious memories we hold.

Brenda Maple

THE HOLIDAY

A place in the sun,
Somewhere to run.
A place to have fun,
The adventure has begun.

A world full of joy,
A girl and a boy.
A world full of light,
The future looks bright.

A break by the sea,
Just him and her.
A break from the norm,
Memories will form.

A dance in the disco,
Slow, sultry tango.
A dance in the club,
Put your hands up.

A place in the sun,
A boy and a girl.
As love starts to blossom,
She becomes his world.

Matt Humphries

LOVE

An electrifying light,
brighter than life,
stuns us into believing,
knowing, that something
amazing, beautiful, spectacular
is waiting.

It runs sparked fingers
down goose-pricked spines.
A feeling floods under, over,
between like it needs
to be felt, seen. It's a vision, a dream
of what could be.

An explosion of colour,
rainbow-tinted
love sparking, flying, firing.
Love like a Tesla coil,
self-made lightning, untiring,
ultimate.

Kerry Summers

LOCAL WOMAN

She has pulled herself up by her own bootstraps
Not at all spoilt
She's a working class, Oxfordshire lass,
She's a gentle, pleasant, salt-of-the-earth character
With a soothing voice
She's a peaceful girl
A nice time you'll have with her
She's great company

So! My lovely
You'll always be on my mind
Part of my memories
I'll never forget you
You always calm my nightmares
How are you, my sweetheart?
May the sun shine on you always.

Mutley

I THOUGHT OF YOU TODAY

I thought of you today
Not as you are now
But as you once were;
Hot in youth
Honeyed in love
And I thought of how we were
Starting out together
Unsure of ourselves
Uncertain of each other
But knowing we were one.

I looked at you today
Seeing the changes that
Time brings, seeing you
Content with life
Settled in love
And I celebrated how we are
Today, together
Sure of our love
Certain of each other
Knowing we are one.

Sue Gerrard

JUST JEAN

Eyes of blue
hair of gold
never in your heart to scold
Just Jean

sweet sixteen
never a care
such fantastic love to share
Just Jean

nothing special
smiles with ease
we hold hands tightly just to please
Just Jean

always together
never apart
first time we met she had stolen my heart
Just Jean

alas fate came
and crossed our tracks
so never again will she join her Max
Just Jean.

Robert Stevens

IF ONLY

I recall the fear of missing you smile,
to catch your eye and all the while,
remaining aloof, too scared to be true,
never knowing if you really knew.
How much I loved you, how much I cared,
riddled with doubts and always scared,
can she love me for who I am,
or does she even give a damn?
Too late I left it, to raise my voice,
and in your marriage I had to rejoice,
for I was glad you were happy on your day,
but I will always love you, that will never go away.

Gareth Greer

ROSES

Twenty-four red roses are given
To show our eternal love
They are given with thought
That comes from the heart
They stand up tall so
Proud and trim
Their perfect folds are deep within
The electrifying colour
Your eyes are drawn in
The sweet smell of their aroma
Magnetically you move up close
My dream, my love,
I'm thinking of
Just like the red rose it's deep
within
I'm blessed with thought
And blessed within.

Shirley Walsh

MORNING AFTER A HEARTBREAK

The sky cries all my tears
while I lie here feeling numb
the rising sun shoots rays of light through
the gaps in my curtains
stinging my eyes as it glows over me
I'm suffocating on a lump in my throat as it
grows larger and larger
I can still feel your name embedded into my heart
tunnelling its way deeper into my pit of agony
your lies and insults swirl around in my mind
dragging me further down into my depression
please set me free.

Terri-Ann Hammond

REMEMBER THIS DAY

Seems so long ago
The day we met
Never let go
It felt like fate
It was meant to be
One simple day
Just you and me

After so long
We met each other
Once more
I loved you then
As I had before
For I always will
And for evermore

Listen to my heart
My soul
It speaks to you
Things I want to say
And have been longing to
After so long
Just don't go.

Joanna Murdoch

I WISH...

I wish my mother knew me now -
How proud she'd be of me...
She'd see that I began to care
(too late for her to see)

She'd feel good knowing what she taught
Didn't fall on stony ground;
Her caring ways and sacrifice
Now through my veins abound

Her gentle and forgiving ways
Bring comfort even now
I've tried and tried my whole life through
To be like her, somehow...

Edna Sparkes

MY LOST LOVE

I know you'll always be there
From morning through to night,
And know you'll never leave me
Even if things don't turn out right.

I know you'll always care for me
Even when I try to run and hide,
And know that you will stay
Forever by my side.

I know exactly how you feel
How it hits just like a knife,
So just know that you will always be
My heart, my love, my life.

Roya Alsopp

THORNEY NOOK

Hot sunny, light night
We listen to the waves of sea surf.
Below sand hill with turf grass on top
Me and fair skinned lass fool around
In the sticky sand.
I could see her perspire
Through her blouse
The silky sand got everywhere
And my hand stroked her leg.
I kissed her lipstick lips
Taste of cherry blossom.
We both lay hand in hand
Looking up at bright blue night sky.

Martin F Holmes

WINTER LOVE

Words whispered softly in winter
A fire burning brightly within
Soul dancing in love's eternal flames
Kisses passionately linger on lips
Slowly cascading down neck
Skin pale delicately bare
A lover's caress
Sparks ignited
Eyes gaze deeply into one another
The moonlight glows from darkness
As unsaid words fill the night breeze
Between two hearts.

Jessica Stephanie Powell

LOVE FAVOURS

Does love return favours?
My white dream told me
To look out for affection
In a vase of heart-flowers.
There will be turnarounds
When eyes of acceptance
Dedicate looks in the language
That best says, 'I embrace you.'
If favours for love rise sun-like...
Then all fine dreams will become real;
Tenderness-starry-skies will sing...
The landscapes and heavens too.

Muhammad Khurram Salim

A POEM FOR MY BELOVED

To my beloved,
'Tis clear to see the warmth in mine heart,
These sparkles that escape from mine eyes,
Mine lips never tire of smiling,
For love has struck me,
Like lightning to a tree,
I feel thy presence overwhelm me,
Desiring thee near,
So the pounding of mine bosom thee can hear,
I feel cherished,
Every time I am with thee,
In thy armoured love.

Sara Nadeen Ashbourne

I AM MICHAEL

I am aware
Of the stare
In the shop
Hold on

Dreams
So slow
In coming
Keep on

I am...
Michael
I call out
Your name

Say it well
I can tell
All -
Who you are

Michael!
Michael!
Stay close
We love you

Yes -
We do!
Love you!
Michael!

Stella M Thompson

BE WITH ME

Be here with me
As still as a mountain
As a cold biting wind on my cheeks
As the sound of the tall rooted trees standing in the glow of the
low autumn sun

Be with me, be with me,
In the silent tiny drops of my tears and the vast space of my heart

Be of me,
And only, only of feelings,
In the dark starless night and be my timeless light.

Kunjan Thankey

REMEMBER MUM

It's many years
Since you were here,
Still I cry a silent tear
For a wonderful mum
So kind and true,
A beautiful mum
Soft, warm and cuddly too.
We'd all come to visit Dad and you
I'll always remember
Your favourite colour was blue.
You were the best mum
We all knew.
Though it's many years ago
We still love you so.

Trudie Sullivan

WARM WINTERS

From your heart to mine, I write this rhyme, expressing your beauty within.
It's a crime you don't see, what I've always seen, it's truly the ultimate sin.
Your silky blonde hair, stunning blue eyes, is really a sight to behold.
But what stands out the most.
Not the looks or the clothes.
You make me feel warm when I'm cold.

André Straker-Brown

WHERE TO FIND MY VOICE

In the words of another,
From the mouths of babes,
Hidden in my scriptures,
A virtual haven text,
Teetering on your lips,
The black behind my eyes,
Through the grass whispering,
While you lay on your side,
Sometimes birds sing it,
Bees and butterfly too,
But where is my voice,
When I want to say,
I love you.

Mark Shaw

I LOVE HER

I love her more than my wildest dreams:
Shattered cream cake on sunlit days,
April honey waxed in pear shaped sways
As I rotate my imagery upon veritable themes.
Dark purple mystery, secret that lies hidden,
Capture the sphinx of lioness' prey,
A divine goddess like rosemary Helen;
I'd rather lose my mind than decay.

Liba Ravindran

MY LOVE

Softy she whispers words of love.
Gentle, her fingers that caress.
How sweet the lips that place a kiss,
She fills my heart with tenderness.
Each passing hour seems more worthwhile,
Each precious moment treasured so.
As I look into her smiling eyes,
My love, what can it do, but grow.

Gary Smith

ETERNAL LOVE

Eternal love of the day
With rays of eternal light
Follow the shadows
Caressing them with love
With warmth
Eternal love of the day
Shines from day to night
Sparkling diamonds
Towards the shore
Cleansing every living pore
Eternal love
That's what it is.

Paul Billett

TWO SKELETONS

Two skeletons, together
Beneath a new world
Hidden below Heaven and Earth
Never to see another sunset
Nor gaze upon a shooting star
Never to feel the icy wind blow
Nor hear the wild wolf howl
Two skeletons, together
Beneath a new world
At rest, at peace, in love.

Ben Connor

I DREAM

I dream
Passage
Of
Time.

Sleep
Hallucinate
I am
A saint

He took
Me
Fast
This is true

Not alone
Am I
Dark night
Fly away

I am young
He is strong
Tonight
We are one.

Stella M Thompson

DREAMBOAT

The gentle bobbing up and down
Lulls me into dreams -
Of your love.

The sound of music around me
Brings a wistful smile -
It's our song.

Don't ever change the way you are,
Envisioned always -
Everywhere.

Jean Aked

A FRIEND

A friend is from above
Sometimes wrapped, sometimes plain
But always filled with love

A gift that you can't explain
They come and go, hide and show
And when everything changes, they still stay the same.

Carla Dible